THIS MAY BE the best-planned workbench you've ever seen, yet it's relatively easy to build. It includes a smooth top of more than 1100 square inches, two vises, and storage space galore. The article on page 98 also shows construction of the wall cabinet and overhead light

YOU'LL BE INTRIGUED when you see what's above, below and all around this slide-out fondue unit. Actually, it's part of a swivel entertainment center made of stacked boxes. Check it out on page 76

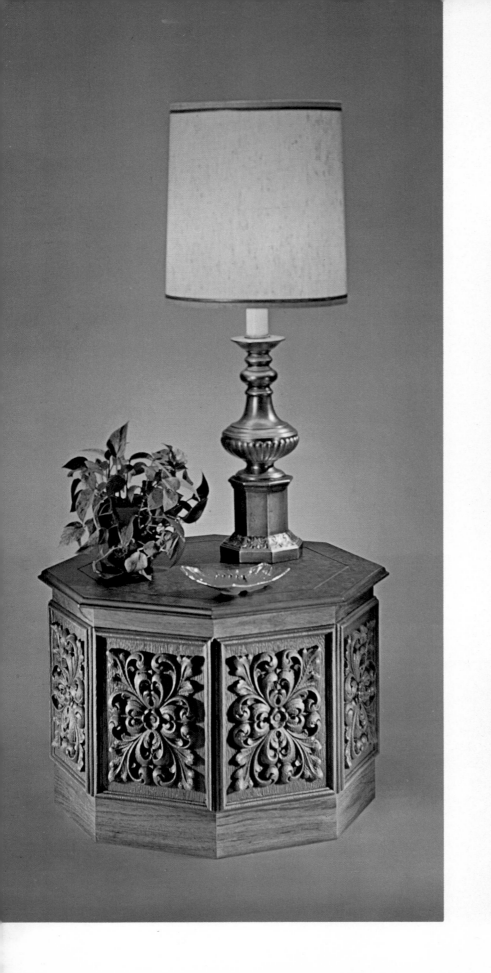

THAT "CUSTOM-MADE" tub-shower actually is a prefab unit, easy to install and clean. See page 4

THAT BEAUTIFUL OCTAGONAL lamp table at the far left looks like it came from the shop of some master woodcarver. Yet it's quite easy and inexpensive to make with molded reproductions of hand-carved panels. Here's a project you'll be proud to show off. Plans start on page 124

YOU CAN LEARN spectacular water-ski tricks from beautiful Christie Freeman (left), champion trick and slalom skier. She takes you step by step through the routine of each trick, starting on page 149. Here are advanced maneuvers that even a beginning skier can learn!

HERE'S A SIMPLE yet highly effective little project that will cheer any room in your house. Fifteen plants in colorful pots give the trellis an ever-changing look as new foliage appears. You'll find the plans on page 90

BUILD THIS DELUXE pool table for $100 (or just a bit more). Complete plans start on page 176

THIS KID STUDIES under his bed! The ingenious arrangement can solve the space problems of a small bedroom. You'll find details starting on page 70

HERE'S AN OLD TWIST to woodturning. You can't really turn spirals on a lathe, but a lathe certainly can help. Learn the tricks of spiral-carving on page 128

Popular Mechanics
Do-It-Yourself Yearbook

1974

Exciting new products

- for your home
- for your shop
- 1974 cars
- challenging hobbies
- new RVs
- gear for outdoorsmen
- what's new for photographers

Great projects of the year

- to improve your home
- shop know-how
- challenging craft projects
- how-to in the great outdoors
- photo projects
- electronics projects
- fun projects

Book Division, Hearst Magazines, New York, N.Y. 10019

EDITOR
Clifford B. Hicks

ART DIRECTOR
Ralph Leroy

ASSISTANT EDITOR
Donna Kalebic

EDITORIAL ADVISORY BOARD, Popular Mechanics
James Liston, *Editor*
Sheldon Gallager, *Executive Editor*
Wayne C. Leckey, *Home and Shop Editor*
John Linkletter, *Managing Editor*
Harry Wicks, *Home Workshop Editor*

ISBN 0–910990–53–0

CONTENTS

Prefab baths are easy to install

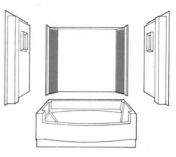

Featuring color-coordinated accessory panels to complement other bathroom fixtures, this four-piece tub-shower has sculptured shelves, a wide rim seat and a slip-resistant bottom. By Owens-Corning

CERAMIC TILE surrounding a bathtub looks nice, but it presents two problems for homeowners: All those grout lines between the tile are hard to clean, and as the house settles, there's the periodic job of recaulking the crack that invariably develops where the tub and tile meet.

Happily, several makers of tub/showers have done something about it and are offering sectional and unitized bath units in reinforced fiberglass. Interlocking sections become a single leakproof assembly, making cleaning easier than ever before and ending crack filling for good.

From a remodeling and modernizing standpoint, these new no-tile tub/showers are made to order for the do-it-yourselfer. Being molded of

Primarily for new construction, the Concept III is a one-piece tub/shower that offers an optional cap to finish off walls and ceiling. By Eljer Plumbing

Ideal for modernizing existing bathrooms, the Versa-Bath will fit through doorways as narrow as 26 in. Strong, rigid and leakproof. By Borg-Warner

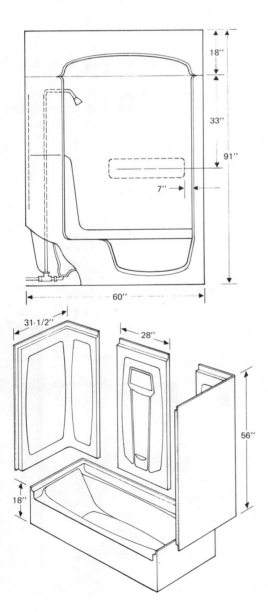

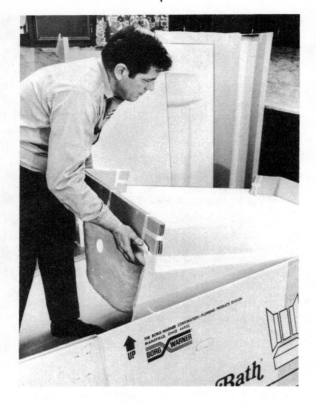

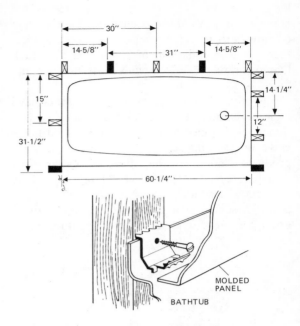

Existing framing requires four additional studs (diagram) for attaching three panels in Versa-Bath system. Barbed fasteners lock the panel

lightweight but strong fiberglass, the tub and wall sections are easy for one man to carry upstairs, through doorways and into place. They can be installed in any standard 5-ft. alcove in a matter of hours with little more than an electric drill, screwdriver and level.

The pictures here show how easily Borg-

Warner's Versa-Bath goes into place. Once the alcove is stripped of the old plasterboard and additional studs are added as required, installation is accomplished in four steps.

First step: The tub is set in place and leveled. A leveling runner on the bottom of the tub permits shimming if necessary. The tub is held with

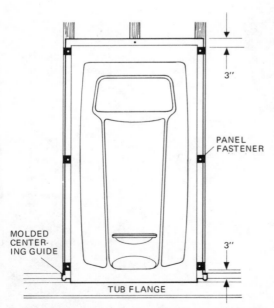

Two guides in the tub flange serve to position and align the center panel on the studs. Six panel fasteners, placed as shown, attach panels to studs

To install the L-shaped corner panel, place it in position as shown, spring it slightly to clear the edge of the center panel and let it snap back

four special fasteners attached to studs with screws. Overflow and drain connections are made and tested.

Second step: The center wall panel is attached to the studs with fasteners and screws. Guides molded in the flange of the tub center the panel.

Third step: Holes for the faucets, spout and shower head are located and drilled through the corner panel with a hole saw.

Fourth step: Finally, the two L-shaped corner panels are inserted into fasteners along the center panel and pressed into place. Top and front edges of the panels are secured to the studs.

Watertight joints are assured by caulking vertical and horizontal seams with mildew-resistant sealant. Surplus sealant can be removed with turpentine

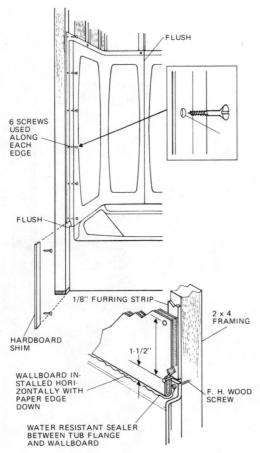

FLUSH

6 SCREWS USED ALONG EACH EDGE

FLUSH

1/8" FURRING STRIP

2 x 4 FRAMING

HARDBOARD SHIM

1-1/2"

WALLBOARD IN-STALLED HORI-ZONTALLY WITH PAPER EDGE DOWN

F. H. WOOD SCREW

WATER RESISTANT SEALER BETWEEN TUB FLANGE AND WALLBOARD

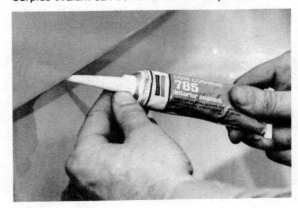

Build a putting green from artificial turf

This synthetic turf is easy to install and durable. It's perfect for laying your own greens

■ IF YOU'D RATHER spend Saturdays swinging a putter than a grass whip, Lawnscape Landscaping is the material that can make your dreams come true. The decorative "carpet" has a fiber facing that closely resembles living grass both in appearance and feel. The beauty of it is that once it is installed, there's no maintenance.

Made of second-generation polypropylene that is polymerized to withstand aging and the weathering of extreme outdoor conditions, Lawnscape is a product of the Ozite Corp., 1755 Butterfield Rd., Libertyville, Ill. 60048. The synthetic turf is sold nationally through carpet dealers and building-supply centers at about $7 per square yard. The same dealers also stock installation materials.

The material can be installed professionally or by a do-it-yourselfer. Since the carpet comes in 6 and 12-ft. widths, the putting greens shown here are designed to utilize those modules.

The dirt or soil subsurface of the area to be covered should be shaped and well tamped. The manufacturer recommends either 1½ in. of asphalt or concrete over the compacted base for the Lawnscape to adhere to. (This minimum thickness will vary with load requirements.) Installation directly over earth is not recommended.

The surface finish should be as smooth and nonporous as possible. Because of the latter requirement, the covered area should be pitched slightly to direct water runoff where you want it to go.

The perimeter boards (headers) can be installed as shown in the drawings (page 10) or as in the photos below. The latter method creates shiplap joints by doubling up two-bys. Start by installing the headers because these can also be used for screeding the concrete. Once they are in and secured by stakes, the earth inside can be excavated and tamped. Then the concrete is laid

Use a notched trowel to spread adhesive on the putting green. When almost dry, the turf goes down

For invisible seams, Seaming Pin-Tape is pressed into the adhesive; the turf is held by the barbs

up to the solid header and maintained approximately ⅜ to ½ in. below the header's top edge. This measurement should be as consistent as possible to maintain a uniform grass height. You can achieve it by using a notched screed on the header boards to level the concrete. If you use asphalt instead of concrete, seal the surface and allow it to dry overnight before installing Lawnscape.

Sweep the surface clean and patch any irregularities. Spread the synthetic turf in the sun to warm it and trim the edges to be butted. Then, using a ³⁄₃₂-in. notched trowel, spread Ozite AP 770 adhesive over the area of exposed width. When the adhesive barely transfers to your finger (10 to 20 minutes), the turf can be rolled onto the surface. You can assure invisible seams with Pin Tapes (see photos, page 9). These are positioned astraddle the edge. The grass is simply tapped into place with a hammer.

Lawnscape and related material—flags, cups and instructions—come as a kit. Simply select the layout you want and order the amount of carpeting in the kit.

In addition to a putting green, you might want to consider the synthetic turf for swimming-pool aprons, patios, roof decks and the like. It's comfortable to walk on and durable.

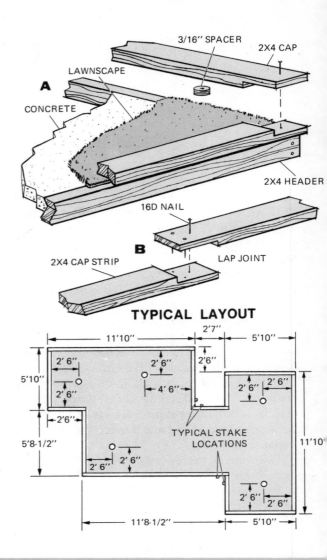

TYPICAL LAYOUT

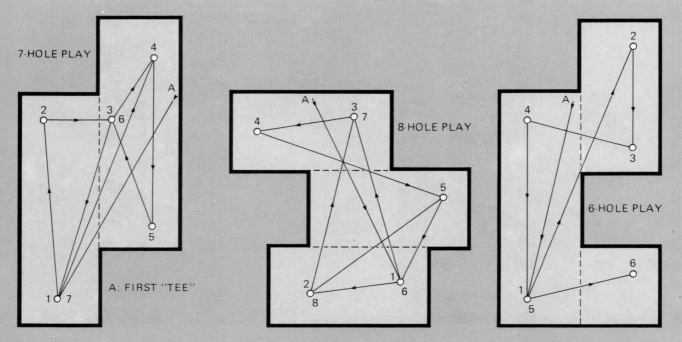

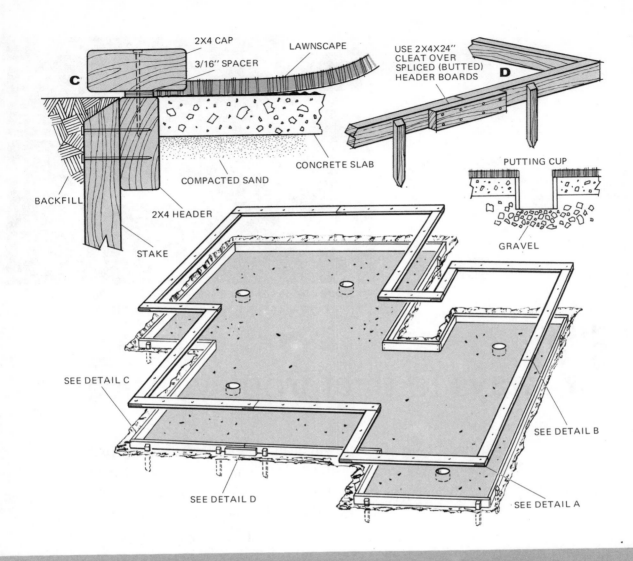

2X4 CAP
3/16" SPACER
LAWNSCAPE
C
USE 2X4X24"
CLEAT OVER
SPLICED (BUTTED)
HEADER BOARDS
D
CONCRETE SLAB
PUTTING CUP
BACKFILL
COMPACTED SAND
GRAVEL
2X4 HEADER
STAKE
SEE DETAIL C
SEE DETAIL B
SEE DETAIL D
SEE DETAIL A

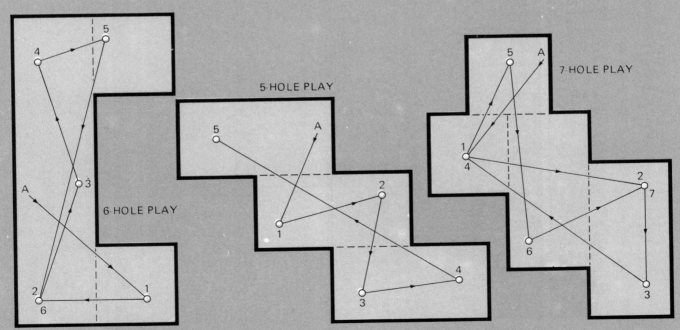

5-HOLE PLAY

6-HOLE PLAY

7-HOLE PLAY

BY FRED W. SCHLUETER

THE ODDS ARE 10,000 TO 1 that any thieves who try to beat this ignition system will get a wrong number. See details on page 18

17 ways to thiefproof your car

Statistics show that the growth in automobile thefts is staggering.
You can take precautions to prevent your car from being
the next one stolen. Here are the latest gadgets designed to
safeguard your car from theft and unlawful entry,
along with several ingenious homemade ways of foiling the thieves

A RADIATOR CAP is all you'd lose if a thief tried to break into a car with this hood lock. See page 15

PUT ALL THESE PARTS TOGETHER and they scream, "Stop, thief!" For more alarms, see page 16

ONE WAY TO NIP mushrooming auto thefts: Replace your car's mushroom door buttons. See page 15

■ IF YOUR CAR has never been stolen, stripped or broken into, it might seem a bit extreme to equip it with all the safeguards illustrated here. But with thieves taking one out of every 99 U.S. cars last year—and with countless thefts from car interiors—it's all too likely that you either have been a victim or will be sometime in the future. And once you have, no amount of theft-proofing seems enough.

So here are 17 types of theftproofing gadgets for your car, with a few variations on those basic themes, and some hints and tips thrown in for good measure. You probably won't try them all at once, but if you do, the odds against your car being stolen or broken into will go up dramatically.

There's a lot you can do to discourage thefts without spending a penny on gadgetry. When you park, always lock the doors, ignition, trunk and windows, and remove the ignition key—even if you're just leaving the car for a minute; the average thief takes just minutes to get a car opened, started, and away. Do this even if your

HOOK THIS LOCK onto your wheel and pedals, and the thieves may not hook your car. See page 17

car breaks down and you leave it to look for help. Just because you can't start it doesn't mean a knowledgeable thief might not be able to.

Don't leave your license, registration, or other identification in your car (unless your state requires it), or you'll help a thief "prove" ownership if he's stopped. And even if a thief doesn't take your car, he may take your registration papers, license plates, or Vehicle Identification Number (VIN) plate, to cover the theft of some other car.

When you return to your parked car, check to make sure your plates, VIN, and papers are intact. You and every driver in your family should also carry complete information on your car's make, model, year, color, license plate and VIN, at all times. Then if your car is stolen, you'll be able to tell the police, on the spot, just what to look for.

take precautions at public lots

When you park in public lots or garages, don't tell the attendants when you expect to be back. Unscrupulous attendants can drive your car away to replace your new, saleable parts with old and worn ones, if they know they have time. When you pick your car up at a garage, check its mileage—a few miles added since you parked it may indicate just such a parts swap. At the least, it means your car has gone on an unauthorized joy ride.

Marking your car unobtrusively won't prevent theft, but it may help you get your car back (and help authorities convict the thieves), should the police ever find it again. A business card dropped in the window slot may be enough. Some owners make tin-can templates with irregular hole patterns, then "fingerprint" parts of their cars with patterned marks made with a punch or nail. This is especially useful in identifying parts of cut-up or dismantled cars. (But be sure to keep the template in order to identify the hole patterns.)

Locking your car discourages casual pilfering. But some thieves will still break in when they know they'll find something of value. So leave nothing stealable where a thief can see it. Even articles of little value may encourage a thief to break in, causing greater loss from damage to your car than from the theft itself.

Transfer valuables to your trunk before you reach your parking place, rather than where local thieves can see you. If you must leave your belongings under glass—in a station wagon, for example, or a hatchback coupe—try to hide the

a hood lock is your first line of defense

STEEL OR IRON STRAP

MILD STEEL ROD

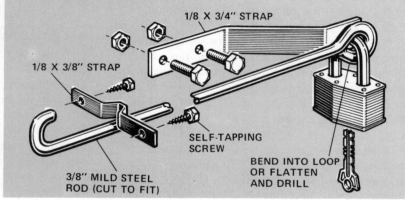

1/8 X 3/4" STRAP

1/8 X 3/8" STRAP

3/8" MILD STEEL ROD (CUT TO FIT)

SELF-TAPPING SCREW

BEND INTO LOOP OR FLATTEN AND DRILL

LOCKING YOUR HOOD will keep thieves away from your valuable engine parts and accessories—also from any alarms, locks or other safeguard devices you install in your engine compartment to protect your car and its contents. The homemade lock shown above is just a suggestion; you'll have to adapt it, or design your own, to fit whatever car you have. This lock is made of a ⅜-in. mild-steel rod (left), suspended from a bracket of ⅛ x ¾-in. flat stock. Another flat-steel bracket is attached to the grille frame (center), and bent so its tip will be near the lower end of the lock

rod, and parallel to it. The bottom of the lock rod can either be bent into a loop, as shown, or flattened and drilled for the lock. Place your parts so the lock will hold the assembly under tension to prevent rattles. Any noise that remains can be damped with rubber hose or tubing. Before you build it, make sure that your design will let you get at the padlock once the hood is closed. If you don't want to roll your own, there are commercial hood locks by the dozens, available at every auto supply store. For three examples of these, see the facing page

thiefproof your car, continued

most valuable under the seat, in the glove compartment, or under less valuable objects.

Eighty percent of all car thefts are made by nonprofessionals between 15 and 21 years of age. Many of these cars are eventually recovered, though often after severe damage (a stolen car is many times more likely to be involved in an accident than an average car). Many more are stolen and stripped of all marketable parts, including accessories, engines, fenders and entire

front or rear sheet-metal assemblies. Even if recovered, stripped cars are just about worthless. And all these are in addition to the cars stolen for outright resale.

You can help cut the toll by resisting suspicious "bargains" in used cars or parts. But it's even more important to protect your own car from theft as much as possible. You can't be absolutely sure your car won't be a victim. But every obstacle you throw in a thief's path will at least tempt him to try some other car instead of yours.

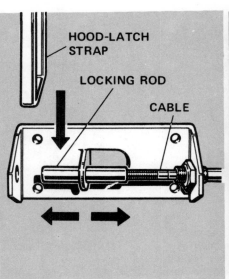
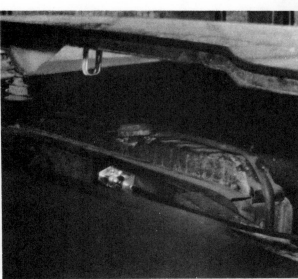

THE IGNITION AND HOOD are both protected with Chapman Kar-Lok. A single button beneath your dashboard shorts out the ignition and locks the hood; a key lock in the button releases it. An armored cable protects both the ignition wire and hood-latch release. Even if the wires are cut, the ignition is inoperative, so a thief can't "hot wire" the system without going under the hood, either. The lock is relatively pick-proof. Thousands of different key patterns are available. The installation is time-consuming, but fairly simple, requiring only a screwdriver and drill. The installation kit includes a lump of clay to take impressions of the space beneath the hood, so you can find where there is sufficient clearance for the new lock bolt. The kit, about $30, is made by Chapman Performance Products, Inc., Chicago, Ill. 60630

THIS CHAIN LOCK will not change your car's appearance because it can't be seen when the hood is closed. It's available for about $5 from Lustre Line Products, Richmond and Norris Streets, Philadelphia

CYLINDRICAL LOCK BUTTONS will eliminate the classic trick of fishing the door lock open with a wire or string (a problem in hot weather when you'd like to leave your windows open a crack). Just unscrew the factory-supplied buttons and screw on new ones

FOR A SPORTY LOOK, these locks appear to be race-car hood pins; they're also a more visible deterrent. They're sold for approximately $8.50 by Eelco, Box 4095, Inglewood, Calif. 90309

LOCKING WHEELS AND TIRES to your car can save you the embarrassment and expense of attempting to drive off without them. Models for most U.S. and many foreign cars are four for under $10 from On-Guard, Gotham Parkway, Carlstadt, N.J. 07072

alarms scream 'stop, thief!' before he really starts

FOR EASIER INSTALLATION, there are alarms that sense the voltage drops that occur when courtesy lights turn on as doors, hoods or trunks are opened; also when the thief starts the car, steps on the brake or even switches on the radio. This alarm has an electronic siren. An optional time-delay switch saves fender-drilling for external key switches. The alarm is manufactured by RFM Industries, Farmingdale, N.J. 07727 and sells for around $40

thiefproof your car, continued

Hood locks are basic to any car protection program. Once under your hood, a thief can easily start your engine, disable most alarms and other safeguards, and steal whatever engine accessories he pleases. Keep him out and you make all your other precautions more effective. Car manufacturers can't provide hood locks due to fire laws in some areas (some do, at least, put their hood-latch releases in the passenger compartment). But if your state fire laws permit, you can choose from a wide variety of hood locks to install—even make your own. In general, the harder the lock is to break into, the more it will cost, so don't economize.

Locks are also available to protect your battery, wheels and tires (including models for outside-mounted spares), gas tanks, glove compartments, and even to lock dune-buggy engines to their chassis. Accessories as simple as straight-sided door-lock buttons can also help keep intruders at bay.

Much as these locks protect your car's accessories and contents, they don't prevent thieves from driving your car away. But locks on your car's controls—or better yet on its operating systems—do help. Congress had this in mind when it mandated steering or transmission locks and buzzers reminding us to remove our ignition keys.

Accessory steering locks are now widely available for cars without these built-in safeguards (or as additional protection for cars that do have them—thieves don't find the built-in kind too

ALARM SYSTEMS won't always stop a thief from breaking into your car, but they may keep him from hanging around to jump the ignition, strip the car or take any but your most accessible possessions from the interior. Some alarms blow your car's horn to attract attention; other, more expensive systems such as this one are wired to sirens. When the siren is mounted under the hood (top), a nearby fender (center) becomes a convenient place to mount the lock switch. Most people mount it on the driver's side to save steps when they enter the car; others prefer the side away from traffic. Switches installed on each door post (lower left) and on brackets under the hood and the trunk lid trigger the alarm if an intruder breaks in. Warning stickers in your window (lower right) may deter a thief from trying, but don't rely on them alone. The alarm shown here sells for under $30. It's made by Ramco Industries, 10 Broadway, Malverne, N.Y. 11565. Similar units from other manufacturers are available at auto supply stores

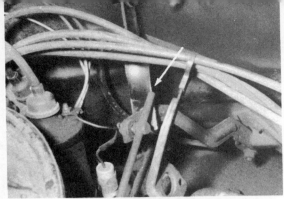

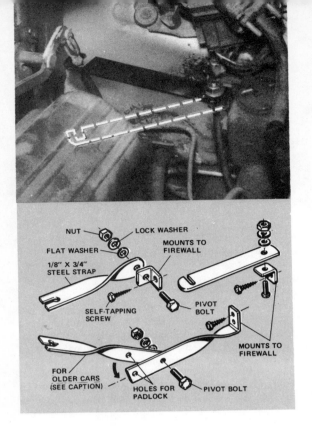

LOCKING YOUR CAR CONTROLS won't keep a thief from looting or stripping your car, but it may stop him from driving it away. The homemade accelerator locks shown here can supplement the steering locks found on today's cars, and thieves will be even less well prepared for them. Hook one over your accelerator linkage and your car won't move faster than its idle speed. A flat, notched bar (above, left), swinging sideways from a bracket on the firewall, will lock many linkages, depending on their direction of movement. Others require an end-notched bar with a half twist (above), mounted to swing down over the linkage. For older cars, where the linkage is so far from the firewall that the locking bar might flex under pressure on the pedal, make the bracket longer and drill overlapping holes for a padlock (left)

a control lock you can make . . . and three you can buy

FOR A PRE-1970 CAR without a steering lock, a rigid bar can be locked over the brake pedal and the steering wheel to immobilize both of them. The Auto-Lok, shown, costs about $8, including a padlock (RMS Electronics, 50 Antin Pl., Bronx, N.Y. 10453). The Auto-Hook Lok with a built-in key lock (not shown here) works in a similar manner (under $14 by mail from Comm Industries, Box 505, Newton, Mass. 02158). Numerous manufacturers have made similar designs that are widely available through most auto-parts or supply stores

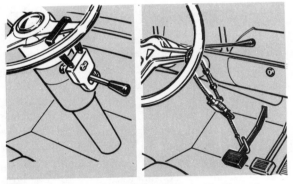

YOUR GLOVE COMPARTMENT can hold either of these steering locks, making them handier than the rigid versions shown at the left (though possibly not as secure). Crowley's Car Lok ($5) fits over the wheel and automatic transmission lever of most U.S. cars, but it won't work in a car with a tilting steering wheel or a telescoping steering column. Brenner Kabe-lock (about $7.50) fits all cars. It coils compactly when you're not using it. You can obtain them from Hamilton Import, 303 Fifth Ave., New York, N.Y. 10016

turn the page

brake, ignition and gas locks

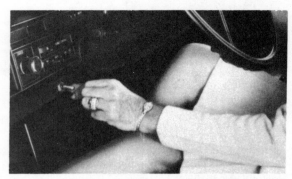

THIS KEY LOCKS your brake system, which immobilizes your car so that it not only can't be driven away, but it can't be towed, either. Since it hooks into your hydraulic brake line, it should also work on trailers—or even motorcycle sidecars—having hydraulic brakes. The dashboard lock uses a special, tubular key (a type often used for alarms, too) that's hard to duplicate. The locking system sells for around $50. Sta-Lok Co., Ltd., 1647 Monrovia Ave., Costa Mesa, Calif. 92627

THIS ANTITHEFT IGNITION SYSTEM is a solid-state electronic combination lock. You can select any of 10,000 different three-digit combinations, yet even if a thief should stumble on the right combination, the car won't start if he's hit one wrong digit. The maker claims this system, which sells for around $90, is virtually impossible to jump or hot-wire. All of the workings are contained in two small boxes. The alarm is by Space Electronics, Inc., Box 634, Littleton, Colo. 80020

THE COMBINATION LOCK shuts off the gas instead of the ignition—which makes it harder to install, but also much harder to jump. The pushbutton console is armored and the control cable holds hundreds of wires, so the thieves won't know which pair to jump. And the solenoid shutoff valve cannot be removed without the right combination. The unit sells for about $160 from Safe-tech, 10 Industrial Road, Fairfield, N.J. 07006

hard to beat). Highly visible, such control locks warn thieves they'll have to work a little harder to get your car than the next one.

Operating-systems locks are claimed to baffle them completely. Simplest of these are hidden ignition switches. Dashboard combination locks like those shown on these pages also serve as deterrents. Other variations include: the Deseko Electronic Lock (about $35 installed, C&W Manufacturing, 235-N Robbins Lane, Syosset, N.Y. 11791), with combination-coded electronic plugs that supplement your ignition key; and the Keyless Key (about $5 from MG Mitten, Box 4156 Catalina Station, Pasadena, Calif. 91106), an ultracompact combination lock for the ignition, which sets off your horn if tampered with.

Blowing horns, flashing lights and noisy bells or sirens make cars—and car thieves—uncomfortably conspicuous. A nervy thief can still work on your car until he shuts off the alarm. But most thieves aren't that nervy.

There are dozens of alarms in addition to those shown here. And now Detroit is offering them, too. Alarms are standard on Corvettes, and '73 Chryslers offer a system built into the car's basic wiring (which makes it harder to detect and disable). The Chrysler unit doubles as an occupant distress alarm—push a button on the dash, and it locks the doors and hood, blows the horn, and starts the emergency flashers. It shuts off after three minutes, so neighbors aren't

"serenaded" all night. But it resets itself, so you're protected.

These alarms are beginning to catch on with other manufacturers. If Chrysler's alarm sells—and it should—other makers are certain to follow suit. The safeguards which today seem so extreme may be standard on the next car you buy.

Try a combination of the ideas presented here. It just might insure that your car will still be there when you return to the parking lot.

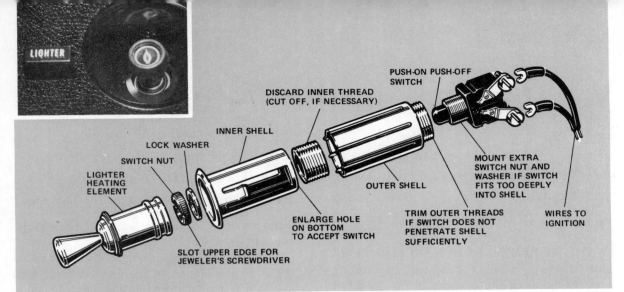

PUSH-ON PUSH-OFF SWITCH

DISCARD INNER THREAD (CUT OFF, IF NECESSARY)

INNER SHELL

LOCK WASHER

SWITCH NUT

LIGHTER HEATING ELEMENT

MOUNT EXTRA SWITCH NUT AND WASHER IF SWITCH FITS TOO DEEPLY INTO SHELL

OUTER SHELL

TRIM OUTER THREADS IF SWITCH DOES NOT PENETRATE SHELL SUFFICIENTLY

WIRES TO IGNITION

ENLARGE HOLE ON BOTTOM TO ACCEPT SWITCH

SLOT UPPER EDGE FOR JEWELER'S SCREWDRIVER

SNUFF OUT THE IGNITION with your cigaret lighter and your car can't be started until you push the lighter knob. The secret is a switch hidden deep in the lighter's body. Connect it between a ground and the negative side of your coil (or vice versa for cars with positive ground ignition); a push-push switch is preferable to a momentary-contact type. When driving, you should carry the lighter element in your pocket, so an unsuspecting passenger won't acci-

dentally stop the car while you are moving. Replace the element when you park. The switch nuts and washers (including the optional ones not shown here) position the switch just far enough into the lighter to be actuated when the element is pushed in. Hacksaw a slot in the face of one switch nut, so that you can tighten it with a small screwdriver after it is inside the lighter's shell. During installation of the switch, the lighter's original inner contact is discarded

baffle thieves with hidden shutoffs

HIDE A FUEL SHUTOFF under your hood, and the thief will be able to move your car only as far as the gas remaining in the carburetor will carry him. Simply install a needle valve (about $2.50 at auto stores) in the fuel line and lock the hood. If your lines are of hose instead of copper, you'll also need nipples and hose clamps. Marine-type solenoid valves ($5) are even more convenient and easier to hide

THE AUTO-GUARD SWITCH disables your ignition, preventing unauthorized shorts even if the wires are jumped. Small, black and unmarked, the switch is easy to conceal and hard for thieves to comprehend if they stumble across it. It fits all cars and causes no battery drain. It sells for about $7 from Raney Sales Co., Box 2112, Decatur, Ala. 35601; Transcontinental Enterprises, Box 191, Kent, Ohio 44240, and many others

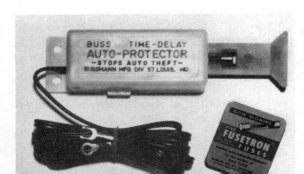

A TIME-DELAY FUSE IN the Buss Auto Protector (and the similar Taroda Steal n'Stall) cuts out the ignition shortly after an unauthorized start. With the car stalled in traffic near the spot where it was stolen, a thief isn't likely to stay and investigate. But you can re-start the car easily. Around $5, from Bussman, University at Jefferson, St. Louis, Mo. 63107; Taroda, 3525 West Peterson Ave., Chicago, Ill. 60645

19

What's what in the '74 cars

From styling alterations to improved fuel consumption, changes are being forced on Detroit. But this was a year to avoid the head-on collision. There are some interesting changes in the '74 models, but more drastic changes are just over the horizon

BY ED NELSON

■ THE WORLD'S CAR BUILDERS face 1974 with changes on every hand. In engineering and styling, from the customer's view and the salesman's, for industrialists and environmentalists, changes are coming. Predictably, some are more welcome than others. But for the most part the '74 models just don't meet the need for such change head-on.

The biggest engineering story has been, and will continue to be, the Wankel rotary engine's move to Detroit. With the advent of the Japanese-built Mazda, rotary engines have been accepted in America. Come 1974, all four major U.S. manufacturers have bought rights to produce Wankel engines. All are secretive about detailed plans, but even the most optimistic estimates see no American-built Wankels before late 1974 at the earliest.

Predictions that Wankel engines ultimately will replace piston engines are common. But Volkswagenwerk AG has raised eyebrows by almost turning its back on rotaries. VW had free access to the earliest Wankel patents and technology, but has announced that a planned new model will have a piston engine. Both Toyota and Nissan planned Wankel-driven cars for fall, 1973, but

neither made it. Both have announced new target dates in 1974.

In Detroit body engineering, Oldsmobile ended 1973 as a leader in using fiberglass-reinforced plastics. The company's Lansing, Mich., plant is the first U.S. car maker to integrate such facilities into its internal car-building operation.

Styling changes for 1974 extend Detroit's tribute (by imitation) to high-status cars from abroad—especially its tribute to Rolls Royce. The well-loved, coffin-nosed Ford L–10 from America's past also has won a salute. And droop-snooted hoods with severely raked grilles remind many car buffs of Italian styling. Other new U.S. cars display a wide, low, sharp-looking front end somewhat similar to the Citroën DS 19 series from France.

The grille most reminiscent of the late Rolls—with stern, upright, rectangular panels angled forward at the center—is probably the Cadillac Fleetwood's. The effort seems somewhat ironic. Rolls Royce Motors, after the collapse of its parent group, recently was put up for sale like any ordinary company. The firm has been patched back together, but workers struck late last summer. They promptly exposed a Rolls project for a new sports model—a low, wide fastback code-named Delta. With a sharply cut-away tail, it is said to look something like Britain's Jensen—a far, far cry from the revered Silver Clouds and Phantoms. Rumor says the Delta will cost somewhere between $51,000 and $85,000. Wow!

Last fall, as new-model time approached in the United States, there seemed little reason to reach even for the *old* Rolls image. Dealers complained that no one would buy the big cars they already were offering. One plush suburban dealer spoke for many in saying, "We're in trouble and there's no way to cure it. It all happened so fast." A Cadillac dealer in Connecticut arranged with a nearby service station to guarantee gas to his Cadillac buyers even if the station ultimately rations gas to others.

Fuel consumption worries probably were the reason big-car sales were in the doldrums late last year.

Plastic front-end panels for new Oldsmobiles are now formed right on the line in the Lansing plant. Olds is the first manufacturer with such capacity

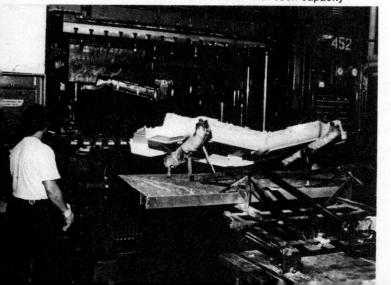

No major changes to improve the quality of either air or water were obvious, but the Environmental Protection Agency (EPA) last August took on the fuel issue. It proposed that car makers tell the gas mileage of their new cars. A label on each would give the figures—the agency's. As its only reservation, Detroit seemed to question the test and calculating methods. Figures would come from a 7½-mile sequence of simulated urban driving on a chassis dynamometer—the same sequence used in testing exhaust emissions. It would apply equally to all cars.

About four months before making its proposal, the EPA revealed mileage data from emissions tests of earlier models. Both imported and domestic cars were listed, but the least thirsty and the most thirsty both came from abroad. A Datsun 1200 got 28.7 miles per gallon; a Ferrari Daytona only 6.3. The EPA itself pointed out that, while figures help to compare one car to another, buyers shouldn't expect their driving experience to duplicate the test results precisely.

Pontiac's Grand Ville is carefully styled to show opulence. Big Pontiac's foot pedal assemblies can be relocated to and fro to alter legroom

Sun roof on the Dodge Dart Swinger tries to give the feeling of a convertible. In recent years, many customers dreamed of convertibles, but few bought

Watch for amber-marker lamps, slightly larger, lower, and farther back. They are the distinguishing visual change to identify 1974 Gremlin X

Buick says its Riviera went through a major change. High-level rear brake and turn lamps are relocated just below the rear window for crash safety

Mazda RX-2 is the world's most popular rotary-engine car. NSU of Germany introduced another rotary in the early 1960s, but it never caught on

The four-door Coronet is the intermediate entry by Dodge in the automotive sweepstakes for 1974. The manufacturer claims a cooler, quieter ride

The 1974 models of the Plymouth Fury are recognizable principally because of the lowered beltline and side windows that are thus somewhat larger

Mustang II became a big-news car for 1974 when it was shortened dramatically, almost to Pinto size. It had won its first interest as a small car

Ford's Pinto, almost unchanged for 1974, is left with a wheelbase only 2 inches shorter than Mustang's. The bumpers are slightly larger than in 1973

Detroit's disposition to co-operate with the EPA (as this is written) seems appropriate; Detroit has just won a long battle over exhaust-emission standards.

The law sets strict new standards for 1975—to become still tighter in 1976. Dates could be delayed, up to a year if necessary, so long hearings were held. Detroit's plaint that the initial schedule was impossible sounded weak against importers' statements they would have no difficulty. EPA refused the delay; Detroit went to court; new hearings were ordered; the delay was granted.

The National Academy of Sciences has concluded Detroit could meet the deadline with the catalytic mufflers it preferred—but NAS adds they weren't the best approach. Academy scientists say Honda's stratified-charge engine is more reliable, burns less fuel, and costs less. Detroit says it is committed to catalytic mufflers. It has won its delay.

In auto safety, the most obvious change in the '74 models is in safety belts. A gentle buzzer is no longer considered a provocative enough reminder to buckle up. If an outboard front seat is occupied, the occupant must be belted or the car won't start. And that goes even if the occupant is only a substantial bag of groceries. But air bags and other passive restraining systems stay on the shelf—at least for the time being.

Despite the advertising hoopla, the '74 models, with very few exceptions, don't really have many substantial changes: a moderate styling departure here, a slight boost in horsepower there, and a required bow to the new safety regulations.

Ho hum. . . .

But '75 looks much more interesting!

1974 grilles—echoes of Europe and the past

CORD?

1

MERCEDES?

2

THE RAKED ITALIAN LOOK

3

4

5

6

ROLLS ROYCE?

7

8

9

10

11

12

13

14

THE FRENCH CITROEN LOOK

15

16

More and more, modern grilles hint of European styling—or of fine U.S. cars of the past. How many can you recognize? 1—Oldsmobile Toronado Custom. 2—Malibu Classic. 3—Camaro. 4—Firebird Esprit. 5—Pontiac Grand Am. 6—Vega. 7—Chevrolet Caprice. 8—Pontiac Bonneville. 9—Cadillac Fleetwood Eldorado. 10—Pontiac Grand Prix. 11—Ford Gran Torino. 12—Chrysler Imperial LeBaron. 13—Pontiac Catalina. 14—Chevrolet Impala. 15—AMC Matador X. 16—Chevrolet Corvette.

Standard travel trailers still sell most, but chopped vans, fifth wheels, motor homes and mini models are becoming much more popular

Quick setup time figures less than 60 seconds for the Coleman Minuteman, a tent-camper-type model that hinges from a low profile to seven-foot headroom

New rigs for roll-along recreation

BY BILL MCKEOWN

Fifth-wheel trailers (with the cargo-bed hitch accounting for the fifth wheel) have jumped from three builders to nearly 100. Below is El Dorado

Pickup camper bodies, like Swinger's new 11-foot Sky Lounge with both front and rear windows, are making camper life much more enjoyable

■ OUTDOORS THIS YEAR, motor campers will head for highway horizons in a broad selection of vacation homes that drive and tow. More height, length and even width are being added to the larger models. The smaller ones feature less set-up time and fewer self-containment complications. Trailer trends favor big fifth wheelers, while smaller models of the booming motor homes chop the back off vans and add on all the comforts of a very compact apartment.

Compact II, (above left) a 13-footer from Hunter Structures, pops top for camping, lowers to garage

Incredibly, there's sleeping room for four in the 13½-foot Love Bug (left). It can be towed by even a small car

Motor homes (above) look less like moving vans. Check this seven-sleeper Xplorer

The Observer is a new penthouse motor home from
Harvest RVs, South El Monte, Calif. It is excellent for
spectator sports or as a rally control center

Riding high, the driver of Shasta's new Motorhome
looks out over traffic. Features include aluminum skin
and frame, roll bars and rubber body mounts

This year, you can expect typical inside features to include running water systems and a
galley, wiring to add outside current, options at
least for a toilet, and any number of heating,
cooling, refrigerating, cooking and lighting appliances as rig size increases. Outside, the new
RVs offer more color choice, better streamlining
and construction to meet stricter industry standards.

As in other fields, standards are becoming important in this exciting and growing industry; a
shopper looking at new RVs should first be sure
the units have the oval Recreational Vehicle In-
stitute seal certifying that the manufacturer has
complied with appropriate electrical, plumbing
and heating codes.

Electric outlets, for example, must be conveniently and safely located, with wiring leading
to properly grounded UL-approved panelboards.
Size of water supply piping is specified, drain fixtures must be individually trapped, fresh-water
tanks need to be of tested and approved types,
and holding tank drain outlets are required to be
accessible and have enough clearance to allow a
simple drain-hose connection. Stoves and heaters

Toyota and Chinook Mobilodge team up to provide
this camper with a push-up built on a 110-inch half-
ton truck chassis. It sleeps a family of four

must be of approved types, installed and vented
so they aren't near flammable materials and curtains. LP-gas piping and joints cannot be enclosed in walls and floors where a leak might
cause gas to be trapped and become dangerous.
Instead, all tubing must be run in the open,
usually under the vehicle, where it is accessible
for inspection and repair.

Here's a travel trailer that hinges down its four walls
to camper-trailer height. The Rolite 1700 has a
power-lift top, toilet and shower

The interior of the Rolite is as comfortable and roomy
as one might guess from the outside. All kitchen
facilities are built-in and accessible

Tri-level fifth-wheeler from Ardon Mobile, Santa Ana, Calif., adds a double bed over a tow-truck cab. The 34-foot unit seems to equal a 42-footer

Ford American Road is the name of this luxury pickup camper. The 11½-footer made of one-piece fiberglass, is self-contained and has two holding tanks

RVI standards inspectors visit member firms regularly to insure compliance. During 1972 five members were expelled for failure to correct deviations from the safety standards, and undoubtedly the RVI inspection system has improved vehicles available and kept the government from moving in to write RV building directives.

Recently, however, the National Highway Traffic Safety Administration, Department of Transportation, has issued a consumer information regulation requiring "manufacturers of trucks capable of accommodating slide-in campers to provide information on the cargo weight rating and the longitudinal limits within which the center of gravity for the cargo weight rating should be located." Pictures of where the camper should be placed on the truck and instructions telling how gear should be loaded will also be required.

standards reduce overloading

Camper builders must also put center-of-gravity position labels on their rigs and weight of unit and equipment, with more data in an owner's manual. Hopefully the new standard will "reduce overloading and improper load placement in truck-camper combinations, and unsafe truck-camper matching, in order to prevent accidents resulting from the adverse effects of these conditions on vehicle steering and braking."

A recent estimate put about 4 million RVs on the road, ranging from $300 tent trailers to $50,000 motor coaches. Travel trailers sold in 1972 alone totaled around 250,000; camping trailers, 108,000; motor homes, 102,000; truck campers, 110,000, and pickup covers, 150,000. Trailers are obviously the most popular RVs, aided by the new boom in fifth-wheel units, and motor homes are growing fast now that less expensive van conversions and chopped vans are swelling the market. Trailer sales increased 30 percent during the year but motor homes were up nearly

Here's a double-duty trailer. All Sports Vehicle from Ace Traveler, Alfred, Me., has four swing-up bunks to allow loading of snowmobiles or motorcycles

Bunks for six and compact car towing are among the claims for 13½-footer by Playpac Industries, Staten Island, N.Y. It even has an enclosed toilet!

80 percent. Shoppers seem to like the idea of an RV with the motor aboard. The big car companies may begin building assorted RVs as well. GM is producing a large motor home and Ford is working with Starcraft on a camper for Ford pickups.

Also on the market are tiny trailers for motorcycles and All Terrain Vehicles (ATVs), rigs that collapse for garaging or open for travel with snowmobiles or trailbikes inside, and rigs to roll-along almost any size family. Americans seem to be rediscovering the out-of-doors. Maybe this year your family can take part in this adventure!

Gear to go for RVs

This top that goes up for headroom and down for garaging is offered by Pop Top Co., Mentor, Ohio, for all van models, including VWs, from 1962 on. The original top can be cut out by sabre saw

For chocking the wheels of a boat, travel or tent trailer parked on a slope or ramp, or for use with any car or RV while you change a tire, the folding Wheel Block from Valley Tow-Rite, Lodi, Calif., is available at most marine and RV accessory dealers. The price is about $5

The Custom Cab, a four-door seating five, is built on Ford, Dodge, and Chevrolet ¾ and one-ton chassis by Tri-Van Inc. for fifth wheeling. A storage box and mid-opening gate are added for convenience

Leveling a camper can be the trick to make a refrigerator operate, pots stay on the stove and a bed stop sloping. The Level-It, Box 4097, Fresno, Calif. is one possible answer. The device is available for about $22, and will help anyone set up properly

No freeze-up in winter, no cycling water spurts, and no damages from city pressure are the claims for this Electra-Flo pump made by Humphrey Products

Bottoming of trailer tail on rough terrain and driveway curbs is prevented by bolting new Skid-Roll on rear skid bars. This wear-saving device is manufactured by Advance Products, Pinole, Calif.

Utility Box Body is the name of this new option from International Trucks. A camper special or a vocational pickup, equipped with the box, offers lockable storage space. These additions also help keep the weight low for good balance with the use of a camper insert

Unpleasant chore of holding tank dumping is made easier with Dispos-A-Hose, Promotional Engineering, International Falls, Minn.

Even a motor home, camper or trailer with a high roof can carry a 300-pound 16-foot hull. Try using the Load-A-Boat system made by American Recreational Products, Lynnwood, Wash.

Riding on air is reported to ease out the bumps for travel trailers. The Hammer Blow Company, Wausau, Wis., provides Air Ride suspension systems for tandem-axle motor homes. The systems also offer easy dashboard-controlled leveling of the motor home at the campsite

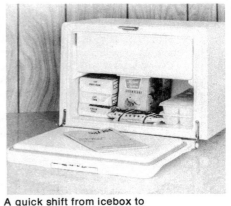

A quick shift from icebox to freezer is possible with a BMC Kardel Freezer Insert. The insert is made by Blackstone Mfg., 4630 West Harrison, Chicago. Ice cubes can be made in 45 minutes inside the freezer

Voltage variations, a campsite threat to airconditioners and televisions, are checked with an inexpensive J. F. Ivan meter

Gadgets for better boating

PAPOOSE is an 8-foot 20-pound aluminum canoe with Dow Ethafoam lining and sponsons for stability and flotation. It is small enough to fit in the back of a station wagon and light enough to portage a great distance, even through the woods. The little craft from Sportspal Inc., Emlenton, Pa. 16373, could prove popular for packing in to remote fishing hot spots. It sells for about $185 f.o.b.

SAILOR SET of rigging knife, marlin spike and fitted leather sheath provides an old salt's complete standby at a relatively low price: under $8 plus postage. Both the marlin spike and the 3¾-inch blade are sturdy stainless steel. The sheath is rivet-reinforced. Goldbergs' Marine, 202 Market Street, Philadelphia, Penn. 19106, offers 6000 other boating items in its $1 mail-order catalog

PACK/RAFT, an inflatable boat for about $120, is from American Safety Recreation Products Group, 16055 Ventura Blvd., Encino, Calif. 91316. It weighs in at less than five pounds, fits in a 20 x 8-inch stuff sack, and blows up to 72 x 43 inches for floating two full-sized fishermen. A wilderness bed, a bathtub, and a shelter are other recommended uses for this versatile little craft. It is made of neoprene-coated nylon which meets all military specifications

FLEX-A-TRIM tabs are claimed to adjust continually and automatically to boat speeds when installed on the transom of any power craft up to 24 feet long. By flexing to water conditions and speed, the tabs are said to help prevent squatting, pounding and porpoising, to raise the hull more quickly onto plane, to improve and level the running angle, and even to reduce the power and rpm necessary for most speeds. From Scott Molding Co., Box 2958, Sarasota, Fla. 33578, the Flex-A-Trim tabs sell for about $17.50 per pair

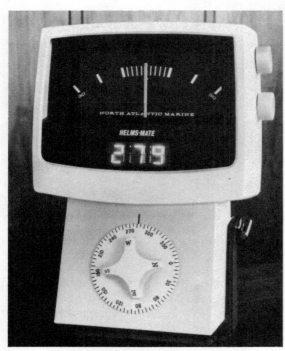

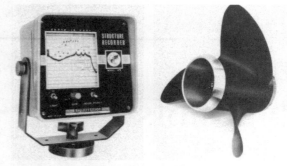

STRAIGHT-LINE CHART RECORDER, Model 470, from Ray Jefferson draws distortion-free picture of the bottom and fish. It sells for about $225

SST PROPELLERS of stainless steel and Teflon S from OMC Accessories are five times as strong as aluminum

COMPASS-HATING SKIPPERS who would give a lot to replace the spinning dial can now pay around $1150 for Helms-Mate computer with digits

SUPER BEACHER slides under a sailing surfboard or a boat and rolls it to and from the water. About $40 from Metadyne, Garfield Heights, Ohio

CONVERSION TO SAIL for any rowboat or canoe is claimed for Michi-Craft kit (about $250), which includes sail, spars, leeboards, rudder and bracket

EXTINGUISHER SYSTEM for engine-compartment fires is FiQuench, a rechargeable unit for owner installation. About $400, from Pike Metal Products

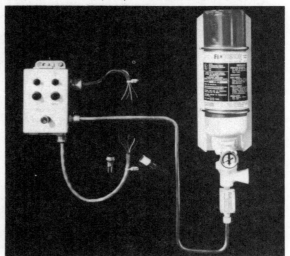

BB guns are big shots now

BY JACK VAN VLECK

For varminting, Crosman's Pell-Clip (left) uses CO_2; Powermaster (right) has a pump

■ DAISY HAS BROUGHT BACK into production that most famous BB gun of all—the Red Ryder carbine. And it's still under $16! At the other end of the price range, there are now $300 air guns that can slap 10 shots through practically the same hole in a tiny bull's-eye at 32.8 feet.

Powderless shooting in its varied forms is enjoying a comeback. With time and room increasingly hard to find, you can't even practice with a rimfire rifle in most suburban back yards. But usually you can with an air gun.

Quiet, short-range economical air rifles and pistols lend themselves to all kinds of outdoor—and even indoor—sports. Backstops such as an old rug or blanket hung on a clothesline, a stump, a pile of grass clippings or a large carton of newspapers make possible such games as shooters' tick-tack-toe, spin the bottle top or burst a water balloon, in addition to target tests. The more powerful arms are simple dissuaders for rabbits who favor your garden or raccoons that delight in tipping garbage cans.

Anyone who has hefted and fired today's finely crafted air guns knows they are not kid's toys, though the economy models are still an ideal present for starting youngsters in marksmanship.

The first recorded air gun was the "Windbusche" made in Nuremberg in 1530, a crude but strong arm with air held in a flask-shaped stock. By 1600 a repeater was on the market, and calibers went up to a whopping .750. During the Napoleonic wars, Austrian infantrymen used reservoir air guns firing 20 shots a minute compared to one-shot-per-minute muzzle-loading powder rifles. When Napoleon invaded the Tyrol, mountaineers picked off his outriders at 150 yards with their nearly silent shooters. So demoralizing were the effects on the French that

execution was ordered for anyone caught with an air gun.

On this side of the Atlantic, Lewis and Clark toted an air gun that could kill deer, while British dandies switched from knife-in-cane walking sticks to models firing air-powered pellets. But early air guns were heavy and mechanically temperamental. Gunpowder dominated. Recently, however, Smith & Wesson reported great popularity for its powerful 78 series CO_2 handguns (exact copies of S&W .22-cal. target auto pistol) in Germany and South American areas where almost no one but the elite and criminals own firearms.

Simple BB rifles and pistols today cost from $6 to $25. Smooth-bored and spring-powered with a simple cocking lever, these are the ones most of us knew as kids. They are ideal as plinking or starter guns.

Next step up are the smooth-bore CO_2-powered BB guns. These are easy to shoot since they require no cocking, and some are semiautomatic, firing a shot with each trigger pull. Replacement CO_2 cartridges are around five for $1.25, with up to 100 shots per cartridge. These guns are in the $25 to $40 range.

In the third category are pump-up rifles or pistols. A reservoir is filled with compressed air from a built-in pump before each shot. These are the most powerful guns, suitable even for small-game hunting or driving away pests. Power is determined by the number of pump strokes so the guns may be used outside or indoors. They cost $25 to $65 in basic models and have smooth bores for BBs or rifled barrels for extra accuracy.

Rifled-barrel air pistols and rifles can be spring, CO_2 or compression powered. They shoot skirted lead pellets (instead of BBs) that look like miniature space capsules. The most accurate of these are rifles with compensating receiver and

Back-yard Dan'l Boones can learn marksmanship skills quickly and practice safely with modern BB guns. Small sharpshooters need an armrest and supervision. An old rug makes a good target backstop

barrel that move back on firing, or with a second piston that moves in the opposite direction to the compression piston.

With adjustable sights, triggers and offhand stocks, competition rifles run $150 to $300. The Daisy-Feinwerkbau 300, Savage's Anschutz Model 250, the Diana 65, Winchester's 333 and Walther's LGV are examples. For $100 to $150 there are the Hy-Score 810M, Diana 60, Weirauch 55 series, Feinwerkbau 200, Walther LG 55M and others. But you can get rifled-barrel models around $35 to $65 for just fun shooting. Pellets are available in .177, .20 and .22 caliber.

Crosman has two innovations of special interest. First is the snap clip of its Model 622. This holds six rounds of .22 pellets for quick CO_2-powered shooting and reloading. The other is the Trapmaster Model 1100, a CO_2-powered shotgun that shoots a load of 55 No. 8 shot to break small clay birds at up to 40 feet. The firm sells a special trap and clay-target set for the gun and the shells can be reloaded. The complete set is about $90 and the gun alone about $50. A reloading kit is under $15.

Today, telescopic sights can be mounted on many medium-priced rifles and make models such as the powerful Benjamin Super Series 3100 or Sheridan Blue Streak really potent arms.

Daisy's famous Red Ryder lever-cocking 700-shot repeater carbine is available again for under $16

Crosman Powermaster 760 pumps up for light or strong velocity BBs and pellets. About $27.50. (Scope optional)

1894 Spittin' Image carbine from Daisy has 40-shot capacity, authentic saddle-rifle look for about $25

M-1 Carbine replica by Crosman, patterned after GI model, has a 270-shot BB clip, slide-cock. About $22

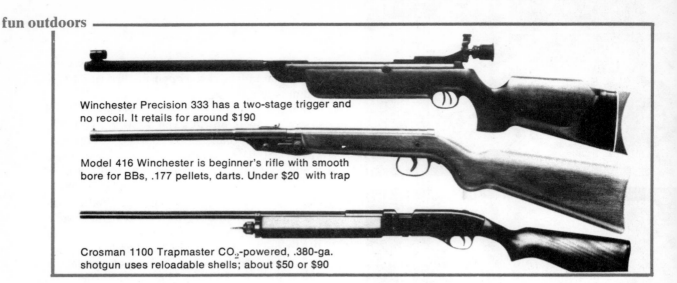

Winchester Precision 333 has a two-stage trigger and no recoil. It retails for around $190

Model 416 Winchester is beginner's rifle with smooth bore for BBs, .177 pellets, darts. Under $20 with trap

Crosman 1100 Trapmaster CO$_2$-powered, .380-ga. shotgun uses reloadable shells; about $50 or $90

BB guns, continued

At last count we noted about 17 manufacturers making hand air guns and 23 turning out long guns. For half a cent per lead pellet and even less for BBs, you can choose from an excellent variety of good-looking models with both indoor and outdoor capabilities.

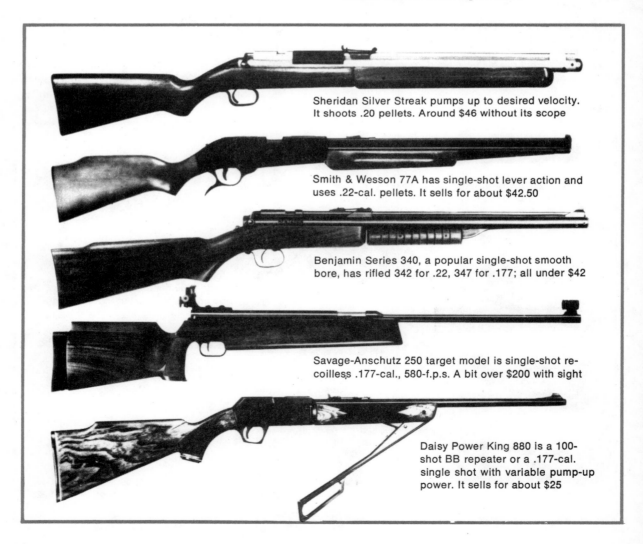

Sheridan Silver Streak pumps up to desired velocity. It shoots .20 pellets. Around $46 without its scope

Smith & Wesson 77A has single-shot lever action and uses .22-cal. pellets. It sells for about $42.50

Benjamin Series 340, a popular single-shot smooth bore, has rifled 342 for .22, 347 for .177; all under $42

Savage-Anschutz 250 target model is single-shot recoilless .177-cal., 580-f.p.s. A bit over $200 with sight

Daisy Power King 880 is a 100-shot BB repeater or a .177-cal. single shot with variable pump-up power. It sells for about $25

New outdoors

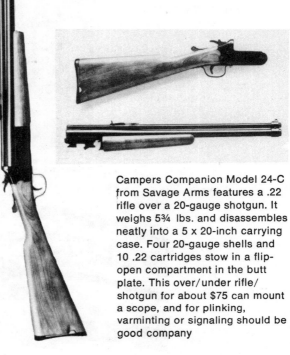

Coleman Lanterns, long standard equipment for outdoorsmen, have now been altered so they hook up with disposable or refillable LP tanks and bottles. They also have been tamed down so that single or even double-mantle lamps can be adjusted from a full glare to a warm glow. Some of Coleman's newer items include adjustable catalytic heaters, assorted sleeping bags with varying thicknesses of Dacron II filling, and Charger 3000—a bright fluorescent camp lamp that runs off batteries and uses an automobile or 110-volt socket for recharging

Campers Companion Model 24-C from Savage Arms features a .22 rifle over a 20-gauge shotgun. It weighs 5¾ lbs. and disassembles neatly into a 5 x 20-inch carrying case. Four 20-gauge shells and 10 .22 cartridges stow in a flip-open compartment in the butt plate. This over/under rifle/shotgun for about $75 can mount a scope, and for plinking, varminting or signaling should be good company

The new camping trend is one fuel source for just about everything. The BernzOmatic Deluxe Camp Kitchen offers a model that converts from carrying case to a two-burner cooking table in a matter of seconds. A double-mantle lantern and distribution post attach to top of the bulk tank

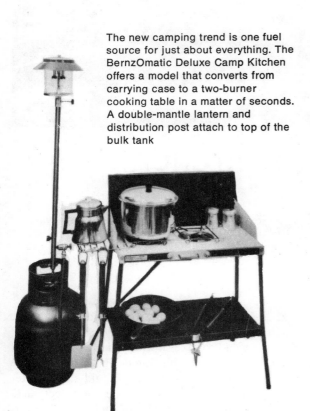

Daiwa fly reels in a new 700 single-action series feature one-piece frames of noncorrosive aluminum, with no screws or small parts to vibrate loose. Large-spool models are reported to handle almost any weight of fly line. Chrome-plated line guards protect the line, and guard and pawls reverse for right or left-hand reeling. The large capacity Model 740 handles up to AFTMA 10 line, 720 for 8 line, 710 for 7 line, and 700 for 6 line. They are from Daiwa Corp., 14011 Normandie, Gardena, Calif. 90247

Take-down bows for archers

A bow you can carry in your pocket? Well, not
quite, but these take-downs are convenient and accurate

BY GARY DENNISON

■ NOW THE NEW TAKE-DOWNS give the archer extra bows for practically the price of one. Bonus benefits include easy adjustment to fit and feel, plus a bow you can almost put in your pocket. Simply by changing limbs on a basic handle you can assemble nearly any bow you want—light 30 to 40-pound draw-weight limbs for learning and target shooting, heavy limbs of 45 to 60 or more pounds for hunting, and maybe a third set of limbs for your youngster to use.

The trend to take-downs was inevitable. Bow-hunters wanted a multi-use design, partly to save money but also because they could shoot better using the same familiar handle for target, field and hunting. The diversity of limb combinations makes the old one-bow archer almost obsolete.

Now you can have the exact bow to fit each situation at a reasonable cost. Usually the handle is the most expensive part of the take-down bow, and if one limb is damaged or twisted, only it will need to be replaced.

With the new take-downs, you spend the usual time becoming familiar with its grip style (as you would with any bow), but once you have it, you have it for good. Attaching a new set of heavier or lighter limbs won't wreck your shooting because, essentially, you will be shooting with the same bow and will be simply adjusting to different draw weights. You'll skip the one-piece bowshooter's trauma. When he switches bows he must get used to a new grip style unless he buys an identical model. The new and different handle can throw his shooting well off for a while.

The take-down handle, however, actually builds confidence and consistency. You'll know how the bow handle feels, how it positions when you make a good shot, and how your wrist and hand set into it for best results. (Even competitive archers do not always realize how a strong, consistent bow hand affects accuracy.)

Compactness and portability of take-downs also appeal to a growing number of bowhunters who travel. Out-of-state trips may include flying, canoeing, horseback riding, backpacking and cycling with the demountable bow packed safely along.

New materials and construction methods are making bows as exceedingly fine, durable instruments for the first time—to be handed down from father to son as fine rifles have been. Archery materials were never as permanent or diverse as they are today. The take-down's structural strength, as well as versatility of limb weights, helps make it a long-range investment.

Many new take-downs have all-metal handles of aluminum or magnesium, specially processed

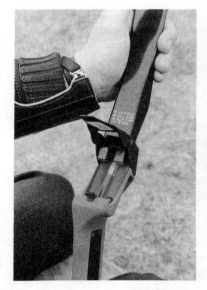

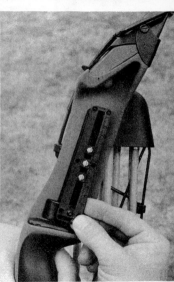
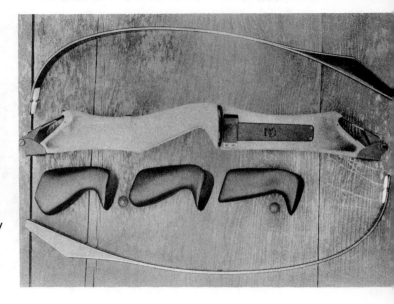

Bows that come apart, like this Bear Archery model, provide a wide variety of designs to match archer style and preferences, as shown on the facing page. The Bear bow (top left), slides grooved limbs into a matching seat in the handle. A pressure latch then is snapped shut to secure a socket-and-latch unit. Options include a choice of demountable hand grips (top right), a quiver that mounts on the bow (center left) and an adjustable hunting sight (center right). A complete set (right) can fit in a travel case that's only 30 inches long.

wood handles, ebonite or composite and metal handles—all stronger than regular wood. Because of added strength, handles can be thinner, easier to hold, and they won't twist (torque) in your hand. More mass weight can be placed near the ends of the handles at limb attachment points, to give better balance, control limb and riser twisting, and damp out vibrations that produced "kick" in old heavy-handled bows.

More centershot—the sight window cut to, or sometimes past, the center axis of the handle—is possible with these new bows. Arrows now come off the string in a straight line, and a bow with more centershot can handle several arrow sizes, including stiffer heavier hunting arrows.

Among more than a dozen different brands, you'll find one, two or three handle lengths, optional grip styles to fit high, standard or low wrist

This two-piece take-apart Ben Pearson bow, made by Brunswick's archery division, joins in the middle with interlocking aluminum knuckles secured by a single pin tightened with a coin

Bolt-on limbs, like those on the Carroll and Wing take-apart bows, are installed on the handle with an Allen wrench

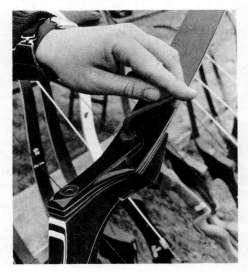

A fishing reel, like other bow accessories, bolts quickly onto an easy-to-tap handle

No fastenings are needed with Wing's Slide-Loc system. String tension holds coupling

Performance is the test for take-downs. SlimLine Competition model bow from Wing grouped an archer's test shots

positions, and several with removable grips. Since metal handles can be uncomfortable in a bare or thinly gloved hand during cold weather, some manufacturers have begun adding leather or plastic grips.

The new materials accept additional drilling and tapping for accessories such as screw-in fishing reels, hunting sights, bow quivers and front-mounted hunting stabilizers. A few have broad-

Stringing a bow with slide-off limbs is no different from a bolt-on or one-piece bow. The handling of take-downs is like the handling of conventional bows

Comparison of a dozen take-down models indicates that once an archer gets used to one grip, he can change the strength of the limbs with better results

head cutouts so you can use same-length hunting and target arrows. Normal riser lengths are 16 to 20 inches, and nearly every maker has two or three limb lengths so you can have a bow of, say, 56 to 64 inches.

Demountable bows can be divided into take-downs and take-aparts. The take-apart concept attaches the limbs with bolts or screws, tightened with a box wrench, Allen wrench or coin. This style is slower to put together but is strong and allows easy limb interchanging. Usually an archer will leave this bow assembled and carry it in a regular long-bow case.

The take-down has the same favorable features but usually takes only a few seconds to assemble or unstring and remove limbs from the handle. No tools, loose bolts or screws are used and the bows are easy to carry knocked down between shooting sessions. Attachment systems usually involve one or two bolts for each limb. On most, like the Wing and Carroll models, the limb is simply laid over the handle and bolted. Others use a metal dowel on the limb which fits into the handle. Either way is good.

A variation is the two-piece Ben Pearson bow. It resembles a conventional bow sawed in half, with the butt of each piece fitted with interlocking aluminum knuckles secured by a single pin. Close milling tolerances provide a very solid fit.

different methods of assembly

The Bear bow has a socket and latch in which you simply slide the limb into a grooved seat and snap the pressure latch shut. The new Wing Slide-Loc involves a tongue-and-groove system, with flanges on the bottom of the triangular tongue and pressure ball bearings which help lock the limbs into the handle once it's fitted together. The Herter's take-down limb slides under a metal tongue and clips into place. Other take-downs, like the new Hoyt and the just-being-released Golden Eagle Hunter, simply slide the limb into a socket and are then fastened tightly with a permanently fitted thumbscrew.

All take-down and take-apart attachment systems have proved safe, solid and dependable. They are closely milled and tight. They won't fly apart should a string be cut or broken. With performance equal to that of conventional one-piece bows, take-downs are popular on archery tournament tours.

Prices range from about $35 to $200, with most about $100 to $175. With today's take-downs, Robin Hood and his merry men could almost have carried concealed weapons.

A plastic injector for your drill press

Strips of tape on the drill-press base provide a quick way of positioning the mold properly each time

Here's a sampling of the molds available, and a few of the many plastic items you can mold and sell

■ YOUR WORKSHOP DRILL PRESS becomes even more versatile with a unique new accessory, called Quick Shooter, which converts any suitable drill press into an efficient injection molding machine.

You just tighten its plunger rod in the drill-press chuck, plug the unit into a 115-v. outlet, wait until it's hot enough and you're ready to mold by pressure countless items in thermoplastic materials in ready-made take-apart molds. The drill-press table supports the mold which is held in a regular drill-press vise (or C-clamp) and the drill-press handle works the injector plunger.

To ready the injector, it must be "prepacked" to assure ample molten plastic down and around the torpedo spreader at the bottom of the heating chamber.

To do this, first unplug the drill press for safety reasons and set the thermostat on the heating chamber a little past medium. Then position the mold so it blocks the hole in the nozzle when the injector is lowered.

When the temperature dial reads 350° F., the proper melting temperature, pour enough plastic pellets in the fill spout and pull down on the drill-press handle. Raise the handle, add a few more pellets and pull it down again. The injector is now ready for use.

To mold a part, line up the fill hole in the mold with the nozzle and pull down on the drill-press handle until the nozzle seats in the retaining ring on top of the mold. Now with a continued steady pull force the hot molten plastic into the cavity in the mold. When it's full, hold the pressure two or three seconds, then raise the handle. The hot plastic cools and hardens quickly and you can open the mold and remove the part immediately. When you want to switch color or type of plastics, the injector is emptied by purging with the block provided.

The kit includes the injector, sample star mold, purging block, nozzle retaining ring, plastic pellets and instruction booklet. For information on additional molds and price of the kit write Haygeman Machine Corp., 2175 South 170th St., New Berlin, Wis. 53151.

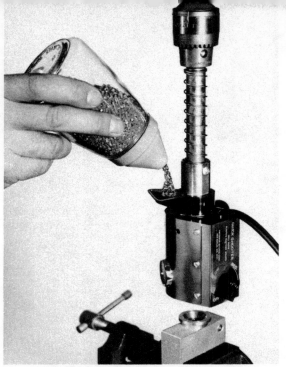

The injector is filled with plastic pellets through a top filler spout. It holds ⅓ ounce

The injector is cleaned of leftovers by placing the purging block and ring under the nozzle

Everything you need is provided in this kit, including a sample mold. Other molds are available

Two-speed belt sander

■ SINCE BELT SANDERS are designed for the big sanding jobs that create lots of dust, having an attached bag to inhale most of the dust (and save the user from doing so) is an attractive feature.

Though "dustless" sanders have been on the scene for a while, the two-speeder shown is Black & Decker's newest offering. Like other collector-sanders, this one sucks up an estimated 60 to 70 percent of the dust. The bag uses the sander motor to do the collecting, and since most of that other 30 percent or so falls to the floor, many home craftsmen have a strong preference for collector-type sanders over bagless models.

Two extremely popular points: The sander's low center of gravity minimizes rocking and reduces arm fatigue during long sanding sessions, and its two-speed feature offers low for better control and finishing and high for fast stock removal.

Bonus: There's a zipper on the bag to make emptying dust fast and easy.

MODEL 7460 BELT SANDER—SPECIFICATIONS

Belt size: 3x24-in.; sanding surface, 13.8 sq. in.
Speeds: 1050 and 1200 sanding feet per minute.
Motor: ¾ hp., burnout protected.
Weight: 9 lbs.   Price about $70.
Maker: Black & Decker Mfg. Co., Towson, Md. 21204

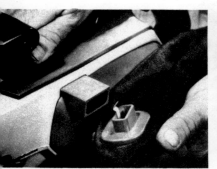

Dust bag (left) is easy to remove and replace. The speed selector is conveniently placed atop the handle. A deliberate gouge in a pine board (right) was created across the grain in only 60 seconds with the 40-grit belt. That's speed!

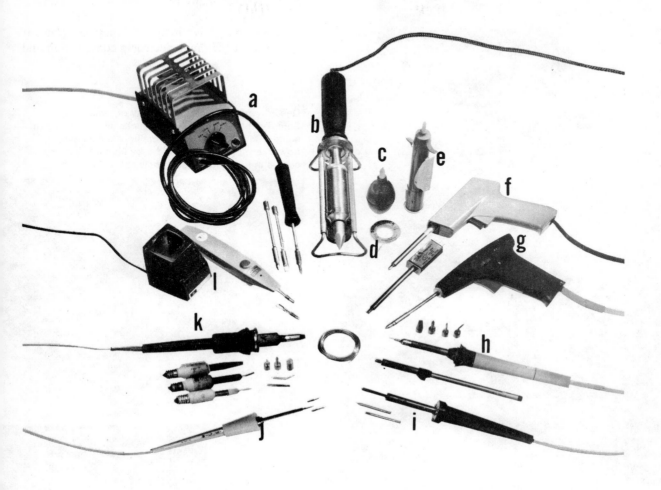

New irons for better soldering

BY JOHN BURROUGHS

A soldering sampler (all prices are approximate): (A) Heathkit, $16; tips $5.75. (B) 200-watt American Beauty, $24. (C) Ungar Solder-Off, $1.50. (D) Solder-Wick, $1.50. (E) Soldavac, $4. (F) Weller Tempmatic, $14.75; Powerhead, $10.25. (G) Ungar dual-heat gun, $11. (H) Ungar Imperial iron, three tips, $10.50; heat cartridge, $5.35; tips, $1.40. (I) Weller Marksman, $3.50; two tips, 85 cents. (J) Ungar princess, three tips, $10.75. (K) Ungar pencil, three tips, $6.25; heat elements, $2; tips, 50 cents. (L) Wahl Iso-Tip cordless with recharger, $20; tip, $2.25

■ NOT LONG AGO, you had three choices when you went to buy a soldering iron: big, bologna-sized irons built for heavy soldering on pipes and sheet metal; hefty, high-powered, induction-loop guns, and stubby little pencil irons with one or two low-powered tips for electronic work.

These irons are still around, but now they have a lot of company: single-post guns, thermostatically-controlled guns and irons, irons powered by rechargeable batteries and low-

new tools

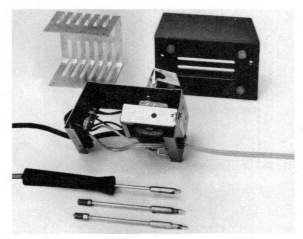

voltage irons with variable-transformer power supplies. The old, original pencil irons now have more tips and elements than ever before. And there are even many new tools for desoldering—a necessity in today's printed-circuit era.

Pencil irons have long been the most popular tools for kit-building, electronic construction and

Desoldering is eased by a variety of tools: Ungar Solder-Off (below, upper left) sucks away the molten solder; its Teflon tip resists melting. Solder-Wick (lower left) blots up the solder by capillary action, comes in four widths, and costs about $1.50 per

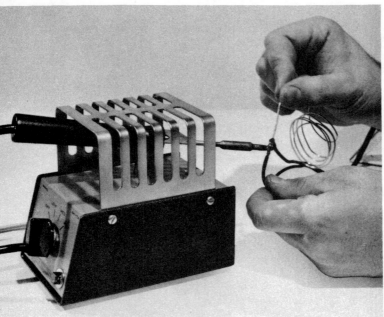

The Heathkit iron goes together in an hour or so. A transformer in the base gives three switch-selected heat ranges and electrically isolates the soldering tip. The cage stand shields the iron tip in the rest position, preventing accidental burns—but it can also work as a "third hand," holding the iron as shown

new soldering irons, continued

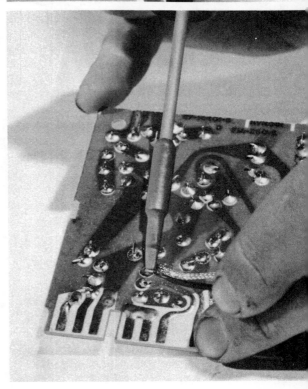

other jobs involving repeated use, since they stay warm as long as they are plugged in. They're also the least expensive irons, with many models costing less than $5.

The first small pencil irons were simple handles, with interchangeable, ceramic-encased heating elements that screwed in like Christmas-

five-foot roll. Soldavac (below, upper right) is a fast, powerful, trigger-operated vacuum, not recommended for ultrafine printed circuits. Ungar Hot-Vac costs about $14.25, is a handy tool that combines a soldering pencil and Solder-Off

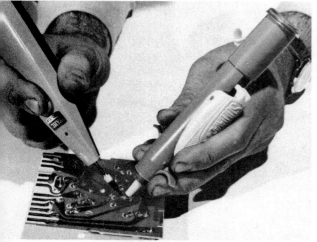

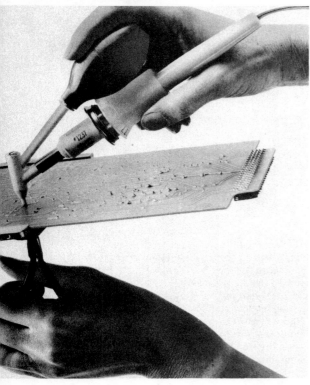

tree bulbs. Some of these elements had built-in tips; others (usually those with fine tips which could be quickly eaten away by chemical interaction with the solder) had screw-in or screw-on tiplets (see photo, page 46) which cost less to replace than entire heating elements. Today, many tiplets are also available with solder-resistant plating, which about doubles their cost but lengthens their lives up to 10 times. Other tips have different household uses, including plastic cutting and sealing.

Newer pencil irons have cooler, slimmer, better-balanced handles, which make them easier to hold, and come with more fine tiplets and fewer heavy ones in keeping with today's emphasis on delicate, heat-sensitive electronic components. Some, such as the Ungar Princess, have elements delivering as little as 10 watts. Other irons, such as the Oryx (not shown) have thermostatic controls which keep the tip within ±4° F. of any preset temperature from 400° to 750° F. Still others, such as the Heathkit, operate on low voltages from transformer power supplies (usually built into soldering iron stands), with switch-controlled tip temperatures.

The transformer-powered irons also prevent damage to integrated circuits and field-effect transistors caused by current leakage or induction during soldering; some regular pencil irons have three-wire grounded cords for the same reason.

instant heat from two elements

Another new kink is the instant-heat soldering pencil from Wall. It's a slim three-ounce design with dual elements. Pushing a switch on the handle turns on the high-wattage element, which brings the tip up to operating temperature in seconds. Then a thermal relay cuts out that element and cuts in a low-wattage element to maintain proper heat with no chance of overheating. When a higher heat is required, the relay cuts in again for as long as necessary.

Because pencil irons are continuously hot, they should be cradled in a safety stand whenever you're not actually using them, so they won't accidentally burn you, your bench or their own power cords. Stands are available to match most pencil irons, including an ingenious American Beauty model that closes like a clamshell over an iron as soon as the iron is laid in place. Continuously-heated irons tend to "dry out," losing their "tinning"—the thin coat of solder that promotes good heat transfer between iron and joint. American Beauty has two answers to that, too: a stand that keeps the iron tip in a pool of molten solder, and temperature-regulating stands (about $25) that reduce the current to the iron when it's in its cradle.

Tip temperatures on pencil irons vary with both tip size and wattage. Among regular pencil irons, 25-watt models with tip temperatures from about 600°–800° (600°–650° with fine tips) are best for general electronic soldering; 35-watt irons (650°–850°) are best for general-purpose household electrical and shop work, and still more powerful tips are best for moderately heavy

work, such as soldering jewelry. For fine electronic work on transisterized equipment, 10–25 watt irons should be used; a 10-watt iron, with a tip temperature from 575°–650°, is especially recommended. More powerful irons are okay if they're thermostatically controlled.

Soldering guns are widely used for heavy soldering (except for very heavy plumbing or sheet-metal work, for which big pencil irons are preferred) and for intermittent soldering, where their quick heating times allow switching on for each connection to be soldered, then switching off again to conserve electricity and prevent tip drying or charring. The first such guns were loop-induction types pioneered by Weller around World War II. In these guns, a very-low-voltage, very-high-amperage current from a step-down transformer flows through a copper-loop tip, heating it to soldering temperature in a few seconds. Heat is controlled by "feathering" the trigger switch, turning it rapidly on and off as the tip cools or warms. But induction guns have disadvantages: They're heavy. Their loop tips

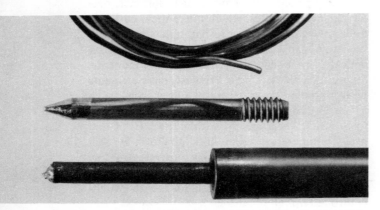

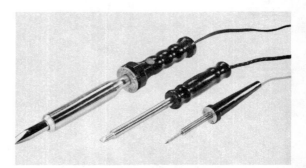

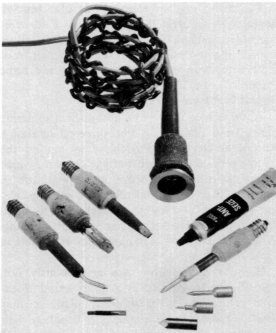

Replaceable tips are a necessity (top) since solder erodes copper tips (especially thin ones) quickly, eventually eroding plated ones. But tip interchangeability also increases an iron's versatility; accessories for the Ungar pencil (above) include heating elements from 27 to 50 watts, tips from 0.056 to 0.395-inch diameters and Anti-seize to keep tips from "freezing" in sockets. Not shown: desoldering tips to contact all pins of an integrated circuit at once

Pencil irons come in a variety of sizes, from 20 to 600 watts, for jobs from fine wiring to heavy soldering of pipes and sheet-metal joints. Since they stay hot all the time, the pencils are best where joints are made frequently, but should be kept in protective stands (above) between joints. Other stands available include temperature-regulating models that reduce tip heat when the iron is cradled, and units that hold the tip in molten solder

are hard to get into tight corners. Feathering the trigger correctly takes some skill. And the heavy tip current can induce destructive currents in some electronic circuits and components.

Newer guns, such as the Wen 450, 222 and 75, and the Weller Tempmatic, eliminate these disadvantages. They're lighter. Their tips are simple posts that can fit almost anywhere. Their tip temperatures are automatically controlled, with no feathering required. And their potential for induction-current damage is lower. They have one disadvantage, though: single-post guns take about 10 seconds to warm up, four times as long as loop models; that's no problem in most home uses, but it makes them less suitable for production-line work.

Weller's Tempmatic gun (about $15) has a ferromagnetic thermostat in its "Powerhead" tip assembly that switches a fast-heating element on and off to maintain tip temperature, clicking audibly as the gun is used. Powerheads are interchangeable, and two are available, both rated at 150 watts: the $3/16$-inch chisel-point head delivers 700° for general soldering, and the $1/8$-inch cone-tipped model delivers 600° for electronic work.

Wen's guns use a different regulating system: a transformer in the gun handle supplies low-voltage current to a new kind of heating element in each tip. The element's resistance is higher when hot than when cold; so as heat is drawn from the gun's tip, cooling the element, its lowered resistance draws more current until the lost heat is restored. Again, changing the tip changes the wattage (Wen doesn't rate its tips by temperature). Wen's Model 450 iron takes 25–100, 100–200 and 200–250-watt tips (about $14); its Model 222 Hotrod takes the same 25–100 and 100–200-watt tips (about $8) and the Soldering Pistol (shaped like a toy revolver) has a non-interchangeable) tip delivering 30–100 watts (about $6).

The cordless iron is another new type, operating from built-in rechargeable batteries. Most widely available is the Wahl Iso-Tip, with 50 watts of output and a tip temperature of over 700° F.

Changing Powerheads on the Weller Tempmatic gun changes tip size and temperature, but not wattage. The 150-watt tip shown has a screwdriver point and an automatically regulated 700° tip temperature

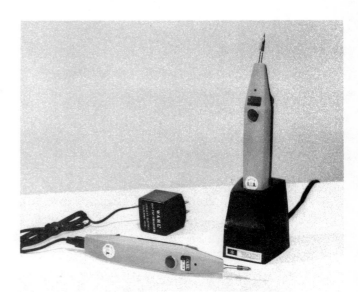

The cordless Wahl Iso-Tip irons store enough power for up to 160 solder joints in a built-in rechargeable nickel-cadmium battery. They have "headlights" to illuminate work. Model 7600 (left) costs about $23. It plugs into a recharger (but can't be used while recharging); Model 7550 ($25) drops right into its recharger stand and lifts out instantly

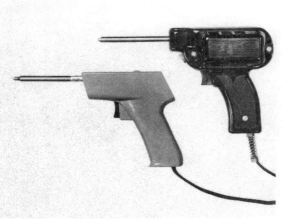

Single-post guns get in tight spots better than older, inductive-loop types. They have regulated tip temperatures. The black gun is a Wen. It takes light, medium and heavy heat-range tips (25–450 watts) and sells for about $14. The other gun is a Weller Tempmatic which sells for about $14.75

■ SAW BLADES with tiny particles of tungsten carbide make cutting most anything easy and Remington Arms Co. of Bridgeport, Conn., has been making them to fit your sabre saw, circular saw and hacksaw. Now Remington has one for your bandsaw.

Such extremely hard materials as tile, slate, hardened steel, glass and asbestos-cement cut almost as easily as hardwood. The endless, smooth-running blade will walk through glazed ceramic tile and snaggy wire grille, and a bandsaw lets you cut thick materials.

These new Grit-Edge bandsaw blades have a gulleted cutting edge for general use or a continuous edge for cutting thin materials. They come in ⅜ and ½-in. widths for 12 and 14-in. home workshop saws and up to 1¼ in. for bigger machines.

'Cut-anything' bandsaw blade

Width	Type Blade	Thickness in Inches	Fine —70 +100	Medium —50 +70	Med. Coarse —40 +50	Coarse —30 +40
⅜"	Gulleted	.025		.047 BS3-2M	.056 BS3-2MC	
	Continuous	.025	.039 BS3-1F	.047 BS3-1M		
½"	Gulleted	.025		.047 BS4-2M	.056 BS4-2MC	
	Continuous	.025	.039 BS4-1F	.047 BS4-1M		
¾"	Gulleted	.032		.054 BS6-2M	.063 BS6-2MC	.076 BS6-2C
	Continuous	.032		.054 BS6-1M		
1"	Gulleted	.035			.066 BS8-2MC	.079 BS8-2C
	Continuous	.035			.066 BS8-1MC	
1¼"	Gulleted	.035				.079 BS10-D2C

Specifications • Nominal Kerf in Inches and Index Number

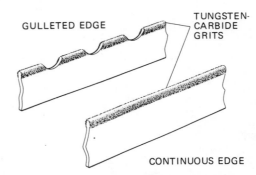

GULLETED EDGE — TUNGSTEN-CARBIDE GRITS — CONTINUOUS EDGE

Carbide blade zips through a stamped metal grille with greatest of ease and without snagging

Ceramic tile cuts like butter with the tungsten-carbide blade, following a straight or irregular line

We test a quiet chain saw

BY HARRY WICKS

McCulloch's new electric
10-incher shushes its way
through all kinds of
logs and branches with ease

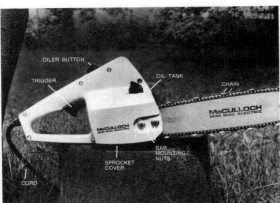

Electric chain saw is designed for comfort of the user,
eliminates messy gas mixing and pouring chores

■ I DON'T KNOW exactly what I expected when I picked up the new Mini Mac electric chain saw. I'm as used to portable power tools as I am to a knife and fork, but not having to yank a cord to get this one going momentarily confused me. But not for long.

After pushing in the thumb safety switch, I squeezed the trigger and the chain zipped into action with no more noise than you'd expect from a contractor-size circular saw. Chalk one up for the McCulloch people; this one is sure to keep the neighbors happy. The 10-in. bar is a fooler, too. It cuts big stuff with a fury. I also used it to prune some dead branches on bushes and in a cherry tree. Here, its size is an asset because you can reach out with one arm to make cuts. Another good feature is the oil sight-gauge. With it, you can check oil level without having to remove the oil-tank cap.

Oil-tank filling is neater if funnel is used. Not visible
in the photo is a thumb safety switch

SPECIFICATIONS

Voltage	110/120 50-60 cycle a.c.
Current	12 amps.
Switch-load rating	25 amps.
Free load	15,000 rpm
Chain speed, under load	Approx. 1000 rpm
Gear ratio	5:1
Oil tank capacity	4 oz.
Bar cutting capacity	10 in.
Chain pitch	1/4 in.
Weight	7 3/4 lbs.
Rim-type socket	9-tooth, 1/4 pitch
Price	$99.95

McCulloch Corp.,
6101 West Century Blvd., Los Angeles, Calif. 90045

A new big-capacity lathe

BY WAYNE C. LECKEY

The big capacity (37 in. between centers and 12-in. swing) allows king-size spindle and faceplate turnings

■ WHILE THE SPECS include such worthwhile features as permanently lubricated ball bearings, a precision-ground steel-tubing bed and an indexing pin for dividing faceplate work, I was anxious to see just how rugged Sears' new Craftsman 12-in. wood lathe would be when put to the test. Frankly, I had my doubts about the sturdiness of its tailstock when mounted on a single-tube bed.

To give it a severe test, I chucked a 36-in. length of 4 x 4 between centers, flipped the switch and watched for tailstock "whip." To my surprise I found that even at high speeds this tubular-bed lathe performed with the ruggedness of lathes costing much more than its price (around $100).

The lathe is equipped with a switch you can lock by removing a novel plastic key, a hinged belt guard you flip up to change speeds and a handy quick-check speed chart posted on the guard.

Two minor things I found "wrong" with the

An indexing pin engages 35 equally spaced holes in the spindle-pulley flange when dividing faceplate work

The tailstock handwheel is turned counterclockwise to advance the cup center. A lever locks the spindle

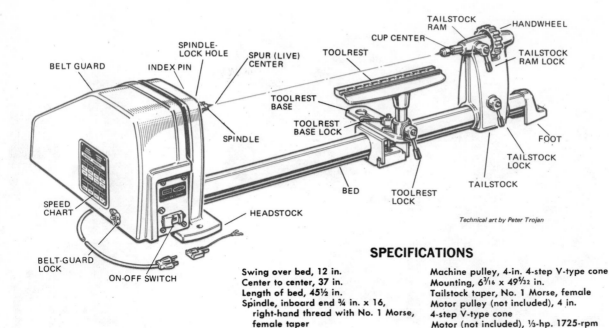

SPINDLE-
LOCK HOLE
SPUR (LIVE)
CENTER
TOOLREST
TAILSTOCK
RAM
HANDWHEEL
CUP CENTER
TAILSTOCK
RAM LOCK
BELT GUARD
INDEX PIN
TOOLREST
BASE
TOOLREST
BASE LOCK
SPINDLE
FOOT
TAILSTOCK
LOCK
TAILSTOCK
BED
TOOLREST
LOCK
SPEED
CHART
HEADSTOCK
BELT-GUARD
LOCK
ON-OFF SWITCH

Technical art by Peter Trojan

SPECIFICATIONS

Swing over bed, 12 in.
Center to center, 37 in.
Length of bed, 45½ in.
Spindle, inboard end ¾ in. x 16,
   right-hand thread with No. 1 Morse,
   female taper
Ram travel, 1⅜ in.
Spindle bearings, two sealed
   radial-thrust ball bearings

Machine pulley, 4-in. 4-step V-type cone
Mounting, 6³⁄₁₆ x 49⁵⁄₃₂ in.
Tailstock taper, No. 1 Morse, female
Motor pulley (not included), 4 in.
4-step V-type cone
Motor (not included), ⅓-hp. 1725-rpm
   split-phase, 60-cycle a.c.
Lathe bench (not included), steel legs,
   2x5 ft. laminated wood top

lathe: There is no provision for bringing the centers in alignment in the vertical plane. They appear to be in a fixed position and the centers of the test lathe were off about 1/16 in. While this would have little, if any, effect when woodturning, it could prevent accurate drilling of work between centers. This slight misalignment, however, may simply be a quirk of the particular machine I tested.

Although they do the job, I thought the locking levers on the toolrest and tailstock were small in size and lacked the good overall design of the lathe, to the point of appearing to be "afterthoughts."

For the $100 price, you get the basic lathe (no motor, motor pulley, V-belt or stand). If you already have a bench to mount it on, you can order a ready-to-run lathe for around $125. A 24 x 60-in. bench with steel legs and particleboard top will cost about $40 more. All prices are f.o.b. Turning chisels, drill chuck, faceplate and work arbors are accessories and priced separately.

Removal of a plastic key from the switch prevents unauthorized use of the lathe. A spare is furnished

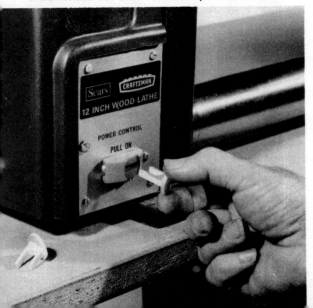

A swing-up belt guard makes it handy to switch the belt on the pulleys for varying lathe speed

A table provides a work stop when the belt is used horizontally. The 4-in. motor pulley drives the 6-in.-wide belt at a 3450-rpm clip

Use try square to check for right angle sanding

'Ugly duckling' sands like crazy

BY WAYNE C. LECKEY

■ THERE'S NOTHING FANCY about this combination vertical-and-horizontal sander. The tilting table has no degree scale, there are no handy knobs to turn for proper belt tracking and tension, and there are no shiny chrome parts. In fact, its welded construction makes it look home-made. But simple as it is, this "poor man's" sander sands like crazy.

Nor does it have a fancy price. If you already have a ⅓ or ½-hp motor you can own this 6-in. workhorse for about $35 f.o.b. It's made by Arco Manufacturing Co., 1701 13th Ave. North, Grand Forks, N.D. 58201, and comes with one medium 120-grit belt. It takes a ½-hp, 1725-rpm motor with a 4-in. pulley. To swing it from a horizontal to a vertical position you remove one wingnut and loosen two others. With the right belt you can also use it to polish metal.

Slotted standby brace helps support machine when swung to a vertical position. A wingnut holds it

Belt tension and tracking adjustment is made simply by turning a stovebolt against idler front roller

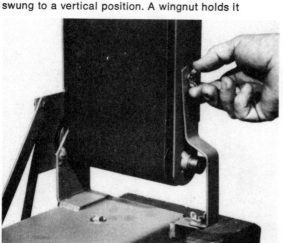

Lightweight saw is a heavyweight performer

BY HARRY WICKS

MANUFACTURER'S SPECIFICATIONS
(Model 961 Circular Saw)

Motor	11-amp., 120-v., 2-hp, 5100 rpm
Blade	7¼-in. dia., ⅝-in. round arbor
Depth of cut	2⅜ in. at 90°
	1⅞ in. at 45°
Weight	8 lbs.
Price	$29.95 (including a calibrated rip fence)
Manufacturer	Wen Products, Inc., 5810 Northwest Highway, Chicago, Ill. 60631

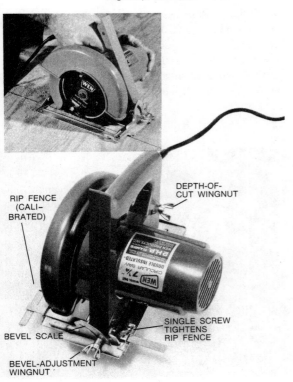

RIP FENCE (CALI-BRATED)

DEPTH-OF-CUT WINGNUT

BEVEL SCALE

SINGLE SCREW TIGHTENS RIP FENCE

BEVEL-ADJUSTMENT WINGNUT

■ WITH THE PRICE of just about everything going up these days, my curiosity was aroused several months ago when a $30 circular saw was introduced by Wen Products, Inc. Since the new saw had more horses and a larger blade, weighed a couple of pounds less and was priced about $6 *lower* than a circular saw that I bought over 20 years ago, I wondered just how well the tool would perform.

To test the saw, I kept it on my workbench a couple of months and used it on those jobs a homeowner most frequently tackles: crosscutting and ripping two-by stock, freehand cuts on plywood (inset photo at left below) and for conventional cutting of ¾-in. stock, including long rip cuts with the rip fence.

I found that the saw is well balanced, easy to handle, and doesn't have to be pampered (held back) when cutting heavy stock. Though some might consider it nit-picking because of the low price, I think it is a mistake that blade-changing wrenches do not come with the tool. I prefer to keep related accessories with portable tools to save trips back to the shop.

To change the blade, two wrenches are recommended; a one-incher for the flange and a ¼-in. wrench for the center bolt (arbor). The bolt, however, can be loosened using just the smaller wrench by giving it a sharp rap on its end. High-impact, shockproof Cycolac housing and convenient location of the saw's key elements (photo, left) are other features that make this saw a good buy.

Flat-top movie projector—a neat trick with mirrors

You simply load the film cartridge in sideways, but the pictures come out upright in this ingenious Kodak system

By SHELDON M. GALLAGER

Pop-up screen (above) makes it possible to view movies right in the projector itself without setting up a screen. With the screen folded flat (in photo at top of next page) the machine functions as a conventional projector. The flip-up mirror throws the image onto the screen, then retracts when not in use. The other photo shows how the cartridge is slipped in sideways, dropping onto a spindle that automatically feeds film through projector, then rewinds it into cartridge

■ YOU HAVE TO SEE IT to believe it. When you first slip a reel of film sideways into this flat movie projector, you wonder how the pictures are ever going to come out right. The secret is a clever system of mirrors that turns the horizontal image on the film into a vertical image on the

To prove a point, the homemade mirror setup shown here duplicates the same optical system used in Kodak's horizontal-style Supermatic 60 projector. Note that beer mug on its side in photo at far left appears upright through mirrors at near left. The combination of two angled mirrors at right angles to each other produces a vertical image on the film. The diagram on the facing page shows how this mirror system works in the projector

lying on its side on a shelf or table and look into the upper mirror. The object will magically appear upright.

Called the Supermatic 60, the new Kodak projector takes standard Super-8 movie film in handy instant-loading cartridges and also provides sound from a self-contained amplifier and speaker system. The smart-looking shallow-style shape is designed to store easily on a shelf and eliminate the height and bulkiness of conventional upright projectors. For quick previewing of films, a small built-in screen flips up so you can see your movies instantly without bothering to get out a separate screen. For group viewing, the small screen folds out of the way, and the image is projected onto a large screen in the usual way. The upper mirror is also pivoted and swings up when the projector is in use. For storage, it folds down flat.

The projector takes the same self-threading, drop-in plastic cartridges that are used in Kodak's regular cartridge-loading upright models. The cartridges are available in 50, 100, 220 and 400-foot sizes. For showing sound movies, the film is first magnetically striped along one edge to provide a sound track, then inserted into a cartridge. You just drop the cartridge flat into the top of the projector and from there on the entire operation is automatic. The film feeds through the projector, then rewinds itself back into the cartridge. Controls provide stop motion, reverse and a choice of two projection speeds—18 and 24 frames per second. The sound system has a power output of five watts and, in addition to the built-in speaker, provides connections for external speakers or headphones. First of its kind, the novel projector is priced at about $460.

screen (see photos and drawings below). You can have some fun trying out the system yourself with a couple small hand mirrors. Hold both mirrors at a 45° angle, one above the other, with the upper mirror turned at right angles to the lower one. Aim the lower mirror at some object

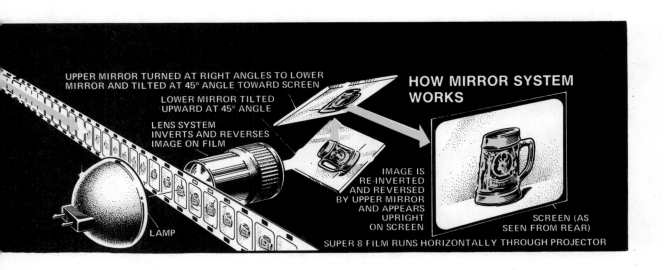

HOW MIRROR SYSTEM WORKS

UPPER MIRROR TURNED AT RIGHT ANGLES TO LOWER MIRROR AND TILTED AT 45º ANGLE TOWARD SCREEN

LOWER MIRROR TILTED UPWARD AT 45º ANGLE

LENS SYSTEM INVERTS AND REVERSES IMAGE ON FILM

IMAGE IS RE-INVERTED AND REVERSED BY UPPER MIRROR AND APPEARS UPRIGHT ON SCREEN

SCREEN (AS SEEN FROM REAR)

LAMP

SUPER 8 FILM RUNS HORIZONTALLY THROUGH PROJECTOR

THE FIRST THROUGH-THE-LENS METER in a production rangefinder camera is featured in the new Leica M5. The meter cell, on a hinged arm, swings up in front of the focal plane shutter when you wind the film. As you click the shutter, it swings down again. The meter scale is visible in the viewfinder, together with a shutter speed scale, viewfinder frames for 35-mm, 50-mm, 90-mm and 135-mm lenses (as in previous Leica "M" models, changing lenses brings the correct frame into place), and a meter battery check. With f/2 lens, about $850; with f/1.4, about $950. The camera is from E. Leitz, Inc., Rockleigh, N.J. 07647

New in photography

FOR SPARE FILM, Klip-Pack plastic cans clip to your belt, camera strap, or pocket. Weatherproof, they float. They can even be sterilized for medical photography; they won't stick to your fingers in freezing weather, either. They are available at three for about $2 from the Kessinger Co., R.R.2, South Bunn St., Bloomington, Ill. 61701

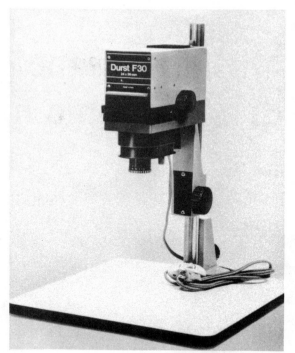

A NEW LINE of five compact electronic flash units from Keystone runs from the under-$20 model shown to a quick-charging, computer-automatic flash just under $70. All models feature color-corrected tubes, hidden sync cords, rear-mounted controls, three-position mounting shoes, and a two-year guarantee. Keystone, Keystone Pl., Paramus, N.J. 07652

COMPACT, ECONOMICAL new Durst 35-mm enlarger makes 11 x 14-inch enlargements on its baseboard. It can be turned to make even bigger blowups on your floor or wall. Color or variable-contrast filters fit a built-in drawer. The enlarger can be taken down in minutes for storage in a drawer or elsewhere. Model F30, under $50. Durst Div., Ehrenreich, 633 Stewart Avenue, Garden City, N.Y. 11530

SAVING MONEY on 35-mm film is easier with this redesigned Watson loader. It holds up to 100 feet of 35-mm film. It lets you wind your film cartridges in daylight. An automatic counter tells how many exposures you've wound. A light trap prevents accidental scratching or exposure. About $16 at camera stores, or from Burke & James, Inc., 33 West Lake Street, Chicago, Ill. 60606

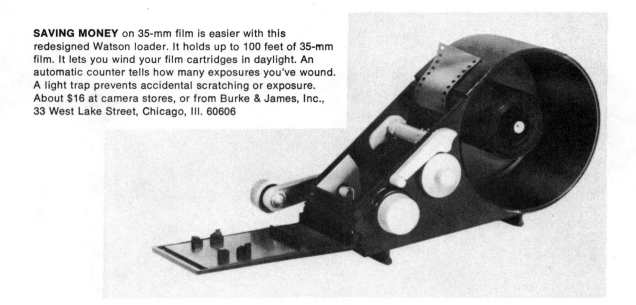

Unsnarling the great quadraphonic muddle

BY IVAN BERGER

Confused about
4-channel systems like SQ,
Q8, EV-4, QS, Quadradisc?
Here's how to tell them apart
—and how to add them
to your stereo system

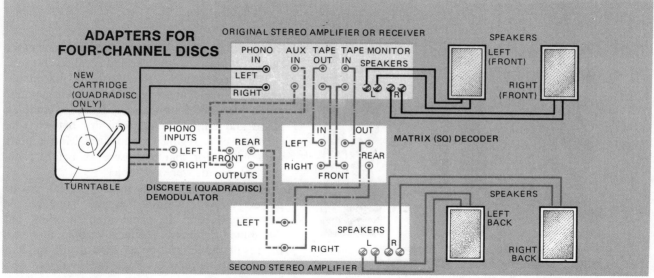

ADAPTERS FOR FOUR-CHANNEL DISCS

Adding four-channel sound to your stereo system is easy. Matrix and discrete systems are shown in the drawing above. Tape decks can be plugged into both of the amplifiers without special adapters

A decoder switch and connections on this Sony stereo amplifier let you control an SQ from the front

Pushbuttons on the Toshiba matrix decoder change the four-channel effects at the touch of a finger. The rear amplifier is built into the unit

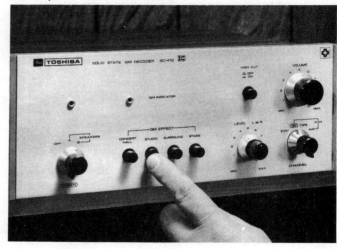

■ FINDING FOUR-CHANNEL systems and recordings won't be any problem this year. But picking the right system could be. Every manufacturer is going quadraphonic—but they're not all going the same way.

With four channels, you naturally get more than with stereo's two: a greater sense of "being there" when listening to concert recordings, more intimacy and excitement from surrounding yourself with music, and more scope for dramatic action in operatic and dramatic recordings.

The big news—and the big controversy—this year is the four-channel phonograph record. Faced with the problem of fitting four signals into the same record groove that had held two, engineers have turned up two totally dissimilar approaches: the matrix and discrete disc systems.

Simplest to make, but hardest to describe, are the *matrix* systems advanced by CBS (SQ), Sansui (QS), Electro-Voice (EV-4) and Dynaco. By manipulating phase and amplitude relationships, they mix four signals into two in a way that permits them to be decoded later. Played on ordinary stereo equipment, matrix discs sound just about like regular stereo recordings. All the instruments—front and rear—are heard, though just through two speakers. To hear these discs quadraphonically, you add a decoder, a second amplifier (which may be built into the decoder) and two additional speakers. (The

Record grooves (magnified 100 times) show differences between the new four-channel disc systems. Stereo grooves (left) carry two channels, one on each groove wall. Grooves of RCA's Quadradisc (center)—identical to JVC and Panasonic four-channel systems—carry left-front and left-rear signals on one groove wall, right-front and right-rear on the other. Decoding information is carried by a 30-kHz signal (ripples in groove), too high to be heard. SQ grooves (right), unlike others shown, are modulated with one signal each; the left groove shows right-rear signal modulation; the other, right-front signal. With four channels playing, such grooves look like more complex versions of regular stereo grooves. They can be played by regular stereo cartridges. Quadradiscs need a special cartridge

quadraphonic sound, continued

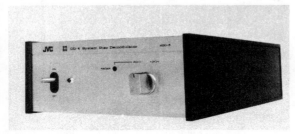

Four-channel converters styled to match other components are available from many makers. RCA Quadradiscs require a demodulator adapter like the JVC unit shown in the photo above. Columbia and other SQ records require matrix decoders like Sony's SQD-2000 (below)

Dynaquad system, though, requires no extra amplifier—just the decoder and speakers.)

The decoder will also produce a reasonable degree of four-channel enhancement (sometimes called "derived" four-channel) from the complex phase and amplitude relationships between the channels of a regular stereo disc. Matrix units were selling for that purpose even before four-channel records were available.

Records made for one matrix system can be played through another system's decoder. At best, you'll hear the same four channels, but distributed differently around the room; at worst, the result should still be as good as the random enhancement you'd get from stereo discs. And Electro-Voice claims its new decoder is "universal," automatically decoding all four channel matrices within two percent of their makers' specifications. In addition, much of this fall's new Japanese equipment will have two matrix positions: one "regular," which Sansui says is virtually identical to its matrix, and one for SQ.

Records are available for all of the matrix systems. At this writing, nearly 100 recordings had been announced in Columbia's SQ system, about 35 in the Electro-Voice system, about 20 to 25 in the Sansui matrix, and a few in the Dynaco system as well (though the Dyna system is primarily sold for enhancement of standard stereo material).

Matrix systems have a big advantage: they can be broadcast over conventional stereo stations, taped and played back, all without losing their latent quadraphonic qualities; it takes only the right decoder to restore the original four channels.

But there's also a disadvantage: that restoration isn't perfect. Mixed with the signals you

Four-channel speaker setups vary widely. Angled speakers here let you sit at a rear wall with proper volume balancing (the front speakers should be louder, so they sound as the nearer rear ones). Experiment for maximum effect

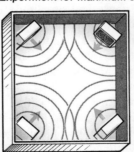
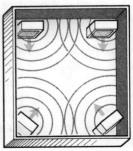

This all-in-one receiver from Toyo has a
"universal" matrix decoder, Q8 four-
channel cartridge player and "joystick"
control with a balance indicator scope

The versatile Panasonic unit plays
four-channel tape cartridges in a car, or
at home through an adapter unit

want to hear in each of the four channels are un-
desired leakages from two or three of the remaining signals. Special "logic" circuits have
been designed to monitor and correct this, but
they apparently cannot restore the full channel-
to-channel separation of the original master tape.

That's where RCA's new Quadradisc system
(actually developed by JVC, who call the system

"CD-4") comes in. The demodulator that sepa-
rates its four channels is controlled by an in-
audibly high 30-kHz signal in the groove. Because it has this extra source of information to
tape, the demodulator is able to separate the
four channels completely. On some recordings,
the difference between this and a matrix system
is imperceptible; on others, the "discrete"

Mid-wall location of rear-channel speakers preferred
by some enthusiasts gives a surprising depth for
rear-room listening. Bouncing the sound off a wall
gives wider dispersion by reflecting the sound waves.
Angle the speakers for the best sound at your chair

Omnidirectional speakers give the widest, least
critical listening area of all speaker types. They can
be used for the front, the rear or both channels. Even
with them, quadraphonic sound perspective is best
when you're not too near any speaker

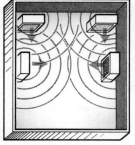
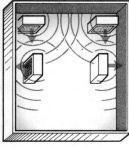
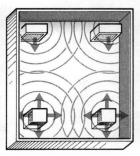
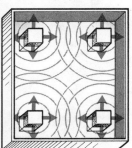

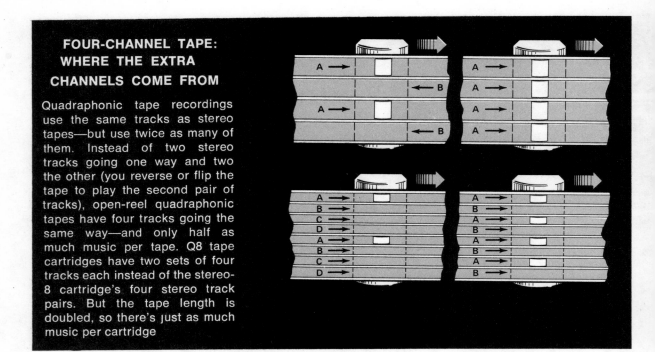

FOUR-CHANNEL TAPE: WHERE THE EXTRA CHANNELS COME FROM

Quadraphonic tape recordings use the same tracks as stereo tapes—but use twice as many of them. Instead of two stereo tracks going one way and two the other (you reverse or flip the tape to play the second pair of tracks), open-reel quadraphonic tapes have four tracks going the same way—and only half as much music per tape. Q8 tape cartridges have two sets of four tracks each instead of the stereo-8 cartridge's four stereo track pairs. But the tape length is doubled, so there's just as much music per cartridge

Quadradisc's separation makes a subtly impressive difference.

But to accommodate this extra signal in the groove, the Quadradisc must apparently be recorded at a lower signal level, making noise (due to dust, record wear or inexpensive phonographs) more of a problem than with stereo or SQ discs. And the Quadradisc's total playing time is barely more than 20 minutes per side, compared to a maximum of over 35 minutes for stereo or SQ.

Open-reel quadraphonic tapes are excellent, but expensive. This TEAC deck lets you record your own

Quadradiscs are also compatible with ordinary stereo equipment (RCA, in fact, plans to offer no stereo equivalent of Quadradisc releases, which will sell for the same price as stereo records). But to play these records quadraphonically, you'll need not only a demodulator but a new cartridge capable of tracking signals up to 50,000 Hz (cycles) in frequency—and such cartridges have already been announced.

Matrix decoders and discrete-disc demodulators are not as closely compatible as the different matrix systems are. Each system will play the other system's discs precisely as though they were the stereo variety; matrix decoders would probably "enhance" the discrete disc, but the discrete system's demodulators would have absolutely no effect on the matrix records.

You can tape or broadcast Quadradiscs, but because the carrier frequency is above the range of most tape and all broadcast systems, you won't be able to receive or play back the result quadraphonically. (And the carrier frequency might create interference on some tape systems.) Discrete quadraphonic FM broadcast systems are already being studied, but it will probably be quite some time before one of them is adopted.

both systems have advantages

Which system to buy? You can make a case for either one. What it boils down to is that matrix discs are more compatible with tape, broadcast and other systems, allow more recording time per disc, and can enhance stereo materials—but the discrete disc does yield a more accurate four-channel signal. And proponents of both systems hope, of course, to find a way around their disadvantages.

Whichever you pick, you can add it to most existing stereo systems easily. Matrix adaptors plug into a stereo system's tape monitor connections; discrete disc demodulators connect between the turntable and the stereo system's high-level (AUX or TUNER) inputs, and the new phono cartridge requires mounts in place of the old one.

What if you buy a quadraphonic disc system now, only to see another system become the eventual standard? If so, you're out part of the cost of your decoder or demodulator—but only part, since you'll still want it to play the records you've already bought for the old system. Your investment in rear-channel speakers and amplifiers (unless the amplifier is built into the decoder) is still good, of course. And most of the four-channel components incorporating one record system have enough flexibility to let you add the other at a later date.

The records themselves, of course, won't become obsolete. Since they're stereo-compatible, you'll always be able to play them, even if you can't always play them quadraphonically.

Tape is a different story. Here, the standards are pretty well established, at least on open-reel and 8-track cartridge tapes. That's because no technical trick is needed to get four channels onto tape—just spread out and use as many tracks as needed. Using one magnetic track for each of the channels, home tapes can produce four distinct signals as easily as the record company's master tapes do. Tape also has the advantage that it doesn't scratch or wear like records do, and that it lets you make your own recordings (though that will probably mean less to you in four-channel).

Open-reel tapes were the first quadraphonic recordings on the market, but cost kept them from becoming popular or plentiful; only about 50 or so quadraphonic open-reel albums are currently available. The decks are big and costly, and (as with all tape) you have to shuttle the tape back and forth to find the selection you want on an album. Threading the tape is also less convenient than putting on a record. But if you're a perfectionist who wants to make your own four-channel recordings, you'll want a quadraphonic open-reel deck in your system. And if you're just

a perfectionist who doesn't want to record quadraphonically, you'll find four-channel decks that just play back without recording, or that just record on two of their four channels.

quadraphonic cartridges for your car

Tape cartridges in the Q8 quadraphonic form are far more popular than open-reel for the same reasons they're more popular in Stereo-8—lower cost and more convenience. Q8 tapes and equipment cost about half as much as open-reel, and the cartridges don't have to be threaded into the recorders. This is also the only system that lets you hear true four-channel sound in your car.

And Q8 cartridges are the most widely available four-channel recordings—so far. At this writing, about 200 Q8 cartridges are available—about twice as many as all quadraphonic discs combined. And the coming flood of discs will probably be duplicated in Q8 form.

As with Stereo-8, with no rewind and no (or very slow) fast-forward, the Q8 format does make it hard to pinpoint the start of the selection you want. And when the special lubricant wears off the tape (though that may take some time), the cartridge jams. But those annoying track-change interruptions have been cut: Q8 players pause to change tracks just once per tape, to Stereo-8's three changes.

Four-channel open-reel and cartridge players can play both stereo and quadraphonic tapes (most Q8 players even switch automatically from stereo to quadraphonic when you push the cartridge in). But if you play quadraphonic tapes on a stereo player, you won't hear the instruments on the rear channels of the tape.

Whether you choose four-channel discs, tape, or both, there are two ways to build your four-channel sound system: by converting equipment you already own, or replacing it with new, four-channel gear.

Conversion may be the most flexible and least expensive method. For a small investment, you can add two speakers and a matrix converter with a built-in, low-power amplifier to drive the new rear speakers. For a bit more, you can get a plain converter plus a more powerful two-channel amplifier. Such converters will let you listen to four-channel matrix discs, to other four-channel sources such as discrete disc or tape (by plugging the demodulation on a tape player into inputs provided), and give you some quadraphonic pleasure from your stereo records, too. Most such adapters have master volume knobs that control all four channels at once.

Those great-sounding new cassettes

BY EUGENE WALTERS

CASSETTE SHELL

SEALED WINDOW

TAPE ANCHORAGE

SCREWS

GUIDE ROLLER

PRESSURE PAD

SLIP SHEET

Features such as these determine how reliable a tape cassette will operate. Sealed windows keep out troublesome dust. Guide rollers and slip sheets help the tape move smoothly. Good pressure pads keep the tape snug against the heads. And a well-made cassette shell helps them all work better

At the factory the cassette parts are simply fed into an automatic assembler

■ NESTLED IN ITS OWN special room in the center of a sprawling factory complex in Hutchinson, Minn., is a clanking monster that covers several dozen square yards of production space. This monster—unveiled in mid-1971 by 3M to a handful of visiting press—has one purpose in life: the automatic assembly of blank cassette tapes. Until fairly recently, it was generally thought that such automation, while not impossible, was still a few years off. The cassette—unlike its open reel counterpart—contains many small components, each of which must be painstakingly assembled into the final package. Ordinarily all of these operations are done by hand, with the consequent possibility of human error.

But automated assembly of cassette parts is just one of the ways tape manufacturers are improving cassette reliability. They're also improving the parts themselves to engineer out jamming and poor tape-to-head contact, and to keep the tape from breaking or slipping away from the cassette hubs.

Even points as simple-looking as the guide rollers (see illustration, opposite page) can generate controversy. The earliest cassettes had simple, molded-in plastic guide posts—and today's cheaper cassettes still do. But the friction of the tape against these posts can cause tape wear or jamming, so most manufacturers use something better—but they don't all agree on

TAPE SURFACE, 15,000X ENLARGED.

Internal guides in BASF "Special Mechanics" cassettes (above) have channelled outer edges to keep the tape winding smoothly and evenly. Spring at rear of cassette is an additional feature found on BASF's C-120 two-hour cassettes

Indexing hole next to the recording-safety tab on BASF chromium-dioxide cassettes will allow future recorders to automatically switch bias and equalization for chromium or regular tapes

cassette tapes, continued

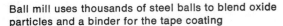

Ball mill uses thousands of steel balls to blend oxide particles and a binder for the tape coating

what that should be.

Sony, for example, uses a straight roller turning on a plastic axle pin. Memorex uses a similar arrangement, with a flange on the roller to keep the tape from slipping off. So do Mallory and Norelco, but with a flange that's tapered where it meets the tape to minimize edge wear. Advent, Ampex, BASF, Maxell and TDK use this arrangement, too, but with a steel axle pin instead of plastic.

In a departure from this philosophy, 3M uses a stainless-steel post which is pressure-fitted onto a plastic inner post. The idea here is that a roller can jam, can get out of line and be otherwise troublesome. The fixed post, because it is a smoothly polished metal surface, is said to offer a consistently troublefree guide for the tape. Also important: The fixed post is easier to assemble by machine.

The slip sheets that lie between the tape and the cassette shell also help the tape move smoothly and reliably. The best slip sheets are plastic coated or impregnated with graphite or

In tape plants, tanks (above) store binder that holds iron oxide particles in place on the tape. The tape comes from the coating machines in 25-inch widths (lower right) for easier and more uniform manufacture. Precision slitting machines (upper right) cut the bulk tape into the desired widths: two inches (shown here), one inch, one-half inch, one-quarter inch (for reel recorders and cartridges) and .150 inch (about ⅐ inch) for compact cassettes

similar lubricant; the cheapest are merely wax paper.

Cassette manufacturers also disagree on the best ways to anchor the tape to the hubs. Many —Advent, Ampex, Maxell, Memorex and Norelco, for instance—anchor it with a round pin in a round hole. Others (such as BASF, Sony and TDK) anchor it in a slot with a two-point clamp. 3M uses a single-point clamp—again, for easier machine assembly.

With the tape moving easily and securely past your recorder's heads, it's important that it contact those heads properly—the pressure pad's job. Some manufacturers (TDK, 3M, Sony, BASF and Advent) mount their pads on beryllium-copper springs; others (Memorex, Maxell, Ampex and Norelco) mount them on springy cushions of foam rubber.

The first cassettes were screwed together. Now, most cassettes are welded ultrasonically, though TDK, BASF, Advent and Maxell still use screws. Advocates of each method claim the other can create stresses that deform the shell

and may cause jamming. However, cassettes that screw together can be taken apart if the tapes jam or break—and if you're *very* careful, you *may* be able to fix the trouble. (If a welded cassette jams, you can pry it open and transfer its tape into a screw-open cassette or into a special, empty cassette that Robins makes.

Improvements haven't just been confined to the cassettes themselves. Tape-makers have also improved the magnetic oxide coating on their cassette tapes, for better high-frequency response and lower noise.

The commonest coating, as it has been for 25 years, is still ferric oxide, a chemical blood brother of rust. But other oxides are popping up, and even ferric has some new tricks up its sleeve.

The big improvement in ferric oxides is smaller particle size. Until about three years ago, the smallest size possible for such magnetic particles was about one micron (about 0.00004 inch) in length. Then along came TDK with its "Super Dynamic" (SD) tape, with a particle size of only 0.4 micron (about .000016 inch) that can be packed more densely and allows more extended high-frequency response. Other manufacturers now have similarly fine-grained, high-density oxides.

Some of the new tapes add cobalt to their iron oxide coatings. But opinions differ as to what it does: Mallory claims that the cobalt dispersed through its "cobalt-doped" tape's oxide coating increases high-frequency response and signal-to-noise ratio by increasing output at the higher frequencies. But 3M claims only that the cobalt concentrated near the surface of its High Energy cassettes increases output overall, with no difference in high-frequency response.

cobalt increases signal level

Other engineers claim that cobalt's only effect is to increase the signal level that the tape can take without distortion—which, in effect, increases the output of the tape by increasing the level of the signal you can feed into it.

Chromium dioxide (C_rO_2) is something else again. Developed by DuPont (which calls it "Crolyn"), C_rO_2 tapes can greatly extend high-frequency response (up to 17,000 or 18,000 hertz, on some machines) and improve signal-to-noise ratio by as much as 4 to 6 decibels.

But the new tapes—especially C_rO_2—aren't completely interchangeable with the old, standard ones. The new high-density, cobalt-doped and chromium dioxide tapes require different amounts of recording bias (an ultrasonic frequency mixed with the signal in recording to reduce distortion and increase dynamic range) and recording drive (the signal voltage applied to the recording head). The requirements for high-density and cobalt-doped tapes are very close to those for standard oxides and these tapes can be interchanged readily; tape decks whose bias is on the low side of the standard tape range may yield overly bright high frequencies and more peak distortion on the new tapes, and decks that are biased to the maximum level recommended for the new tapes will show a slight fall-off in high-frequency response when recording on the older varieties. But the differences are small. At worst, a tape deck set up for ordinary tapes won't let the new premium types deliver all the extra performance you buy them for—though they may deliver some of that performance anyway.

But again, chromium dioxide is an exception; for best results, cassette recorders should be specially designed for use with C_rO_2, with a switch converting them from chromium to normal tapes.

That switch may change not only recording bias and recording drive, but erase current and equalization as well.

All tapes require some equalization—primarily a treble boost in recording, and a more or less equal but opposite boost in playback, plus a slight playback boost at the extreme top end. Since C_rO_2 has more high-frequency output than iron oxide tapes, this standard equalization setup will produce recordings with overemphasized highs. That's not too bad. By turning down your treble control in playback, you'll hear reasonably flat response again, and get lower noise and better overload resistance, too. But using a recorder that's equalized for chromium is even better.

Some recording manufacturers—chiefly Sony and TEAC—change their recording equalization for C_rO_2. Using less high-frequency boost, they get recordings that will play back "flat" on normally equalized machines, and take full advantage of the tape's greater resistance to high-frequency overload distortion. But most manufacturers change their playback equalization instead, using normal recording equalization but reducing the top-end playback boost. This approach—which has now been adopted as an international standard for chromium tapes—trades some (but not all) of that greater overload resistance for an improved signal-to-noise ratio.

hard to choose best cassette

With all the new improvements in cassette tapes and construction, finding a good cassette is easier than ever before. But, with so many to choose from, finding the best cassette for you is harder than ever before. Ask around among your friends who use cassettes and you can get a pretty good idea of whose cassettes are most reliable and jamproof. But their comments, or even published test reports, are only a rough guide to the tapes that will give you the best recorded quality. The tape is only half the story; your recorder is the other half. Because recorder characteristics vary, a given tape will perform differently on different machines. And you may prefer a different balance of tape characteristics (frequency response, signal-to-noise ratio, overload distortion resistance) than your neighbor.

With today's supertapes, when you find the right one, you may hear better performance than you ever thought your old cassette machine could give.

SECTION 2

GREAT PROJECTS OF THE YEAR

On the following pages you'll find the finest of the famous Popular Mechanics *projects:*

Projects to improve your home
Projects to challenge your craftsmanship
Photo projects
Electronics projects
Projects just for fun

You'll also find how-to information in related fields:

Shop know-how
Tool techniques
How-to tips for the great outdoors

Turn the page to find the first article on home improvement—and go on from there!

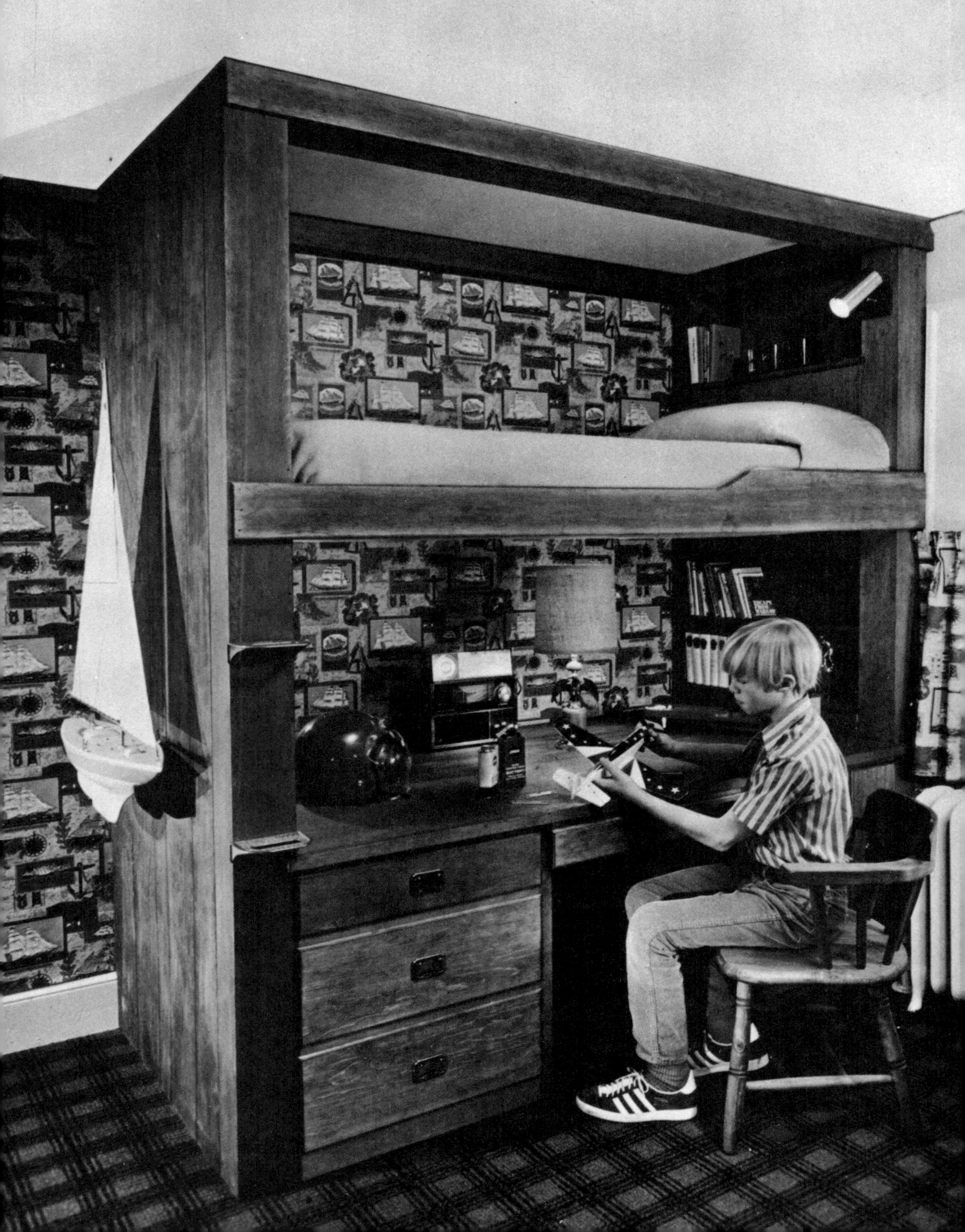

This kid studies under his bed

Here's a novel solution to a space problem in a small bedroom. This combination bunk bed/desk gives room for sleep or study

■ NOT ONLY DOES this kid study under his bed, he sleeps over his desk. Far from being a mixed-up kid, he thinks he has the grooviest bunk bed/desk ever. This combination unit solves the space problem in a small room.

The two-in-one unit occupies a corner of the room from floor to ceiling to provide a regulation-size bunk bed and a kneehole desk with nearly a 4x7 ft. top. Ample in size for homework galore, the desk also presents a great hobby and play surface for model building, train and racing-car layouts—you name it. Three roomy drawers flank each side of the kneehole with a pencil drawer above.

Constructed of common white pine, the unit is pretty much a duplicate each side of a centerline. Like members are made the same except for be-

ing assembled left and right hand. This is particularly true when making the four hollow posts and the two separate drawer compartments.

Since the posts butt against the ceiling they have to be built in place. You can't expect to tip them up into place if put together on the floor. Each pair of end posts is joined with a panel of ¼-in. plywood, which can be plain or fancy with random grooves. If the bed is built in a corner, only the exposed end would require fancy plywood. If centered on a wall, both ends would be exposed. The distance between posts is set by the length of the steel bedrails. The original rails (and mattress) are from Sears and measure 75 in. long. They are for bunk beds without springs, and a pair costs about $6. After the rails are bolted to the posts of each end assembly, you

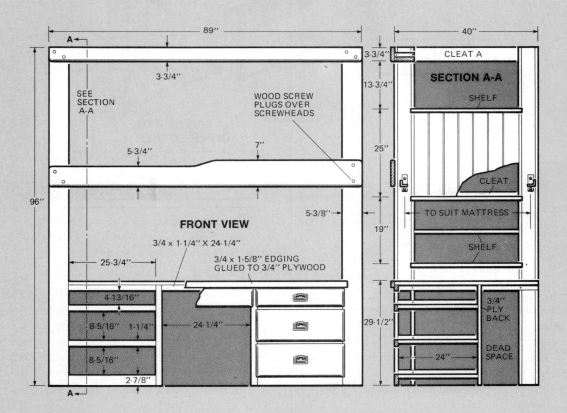

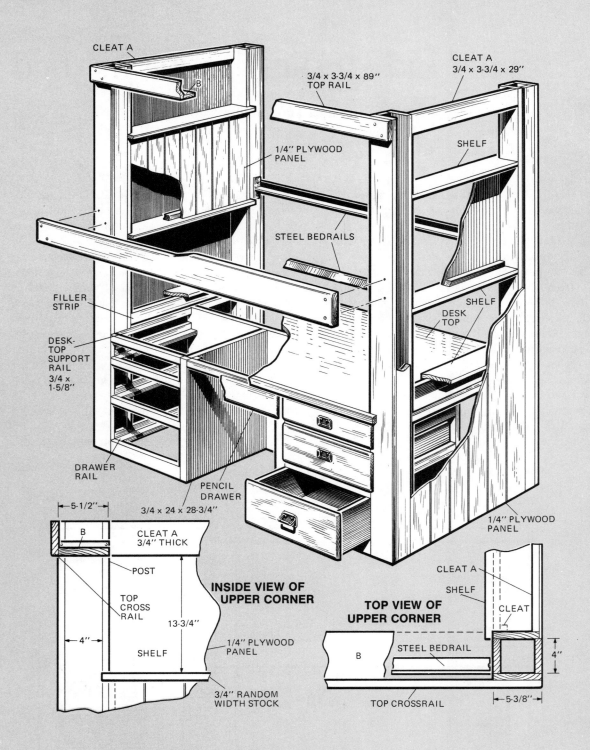

CLEAT A

B

3/4 x 3-3/4 x 89''
TOP RAIL

CLEAT A
3/4 x 3-3/4 x 29''

SHELF

1/4'' PLYWOOD
PANEL

STEEL BEDRAILS

SHELF

DESK
TOP

FILLER
STRIP

DESK-
TOP
SUPPORT
RAIL
3/4 x
1-5/8''

DRAWER
RAIL

PENCIL
DRAWER

3/4 x 24 x 28-3/4''

1/4'' PLYWOOD
PANEL

5-1/2''

B

CLEAT A
3/4'' THICK

POST

TOP
CROSS
RAIL

**INSIDE VIEW OF
UPPER CORNER**

13-3/4''

1/4'' PLYWOOD
PANEL

4''

SHELF

3/4'' RANDOM
WIDTH STOCK

CLEAT A

SHELF

CLEAT

**TOP VIEW OF
UPPER CORNER**

B

STEEL BEDRAIL

4''

TOP CROSSRAIL

5-3/8''

can proceed to add the connecting board across the top at the ceiling and the board that hides the bed rail. These are fastened with screws set in counterbored holes and capped with plugs.

The rails of the drawer compartments are attached to the front posts with dowels. Notice that a full-length plywood panel provides a back for each compartment and the kneehole. This panel also supports the outside drawer slides at the rear.

Make any minor adjustments to the dimensions to fit your particular situation. When construction is complete, the unit is ready for finishing to match the decor of the room.

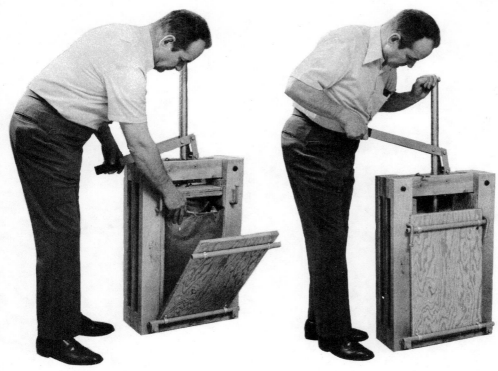

Practical compactor is filled by tilting open the removable door and placing trash in the bag above. The author leaves his masher beside the garbage cans for use primarily on bottles and paper

Door is locked before the pressure foot is pushed down. Silicone spray or wax is recommended on the bag-space surfaces to reduce friction and to give waterproofing in case of trash leakage

Homebuilt masher puts squeeze on trash

BY R. S. HEDIN

■ WHEN I LEARNED that commercial trash compactors cost something like $200, I decided to make my own and pocket the savings. It's not as fancy as the manufactured models, but it does the job. In fact, my out-of-pocket expenses for building it were about $15.

The masher is designed to be kept near the garbage cans, and its operating cost is low because ordinary supermarket bags are used, not special ones. The masher even crushes cans and light bottles if they're laid on their sides.

The force multiplication is about seven times from the handle to the pressure foot, so a 200-pound man can exert quite a bit of force on the trash inside.

The frame is easy to assemble if the corresponding 2x4 parts are cut accurately to length, then drilled with a fixture in a drill press to make all the hole locations exactly the same. Stack the pieces on ½-in. bolts, gluing each joint. After stacking, square up the frame and tighten the bolts, then you can glue and nail the plywood in place.

Use ample grease on the pivot bolts and make certain that the pawl pivots freely when you're assembling the linkage. And finally, apply a silicone spray or a paste wax on all surfaces of the bag space to reduce friction.

To use the squasher, simply put in the trash bag and lock the door. Pull the gate hook and

Typical load of trash after squeezing by the author.
The door and paint were left off this prototype
masher for the photo. Builders are advised to complete mashers by painting with quality exterior paint

homebuilt masher, continued

Here is a close-up view of the pressure mechanism
assembly. Note that an ordinary gatehook is used to
hold the pressure foot up

As shown in this rear-view photo of the masher the
back is attached using lagscrews and bolts about 14
in. long. The masher shown utilizes typical
supermarket bags that every housewife gets her
groceries in. The manufactured compactors require
costly commercial bags. You will save money initially
—and every time you mash!

push the pressure foot down. As you push the
handle it causes the pawl to engage one of the
notches in the pipe. You raise the handle to release the pressure and raise the pawl in position
so you can catch a higher pipe-notch. Pump the
handle several times to compress the trash and
hold down on the lifting handle when raising the
pressure handle because there will usually be
some spring-back.

When the trash is compacted, release the pressure, lift the pawl rod to a horizontal position and
raise the pressure foot. Engage the gate hook to
hold the foot up, open the door and remove the
compacted trash.

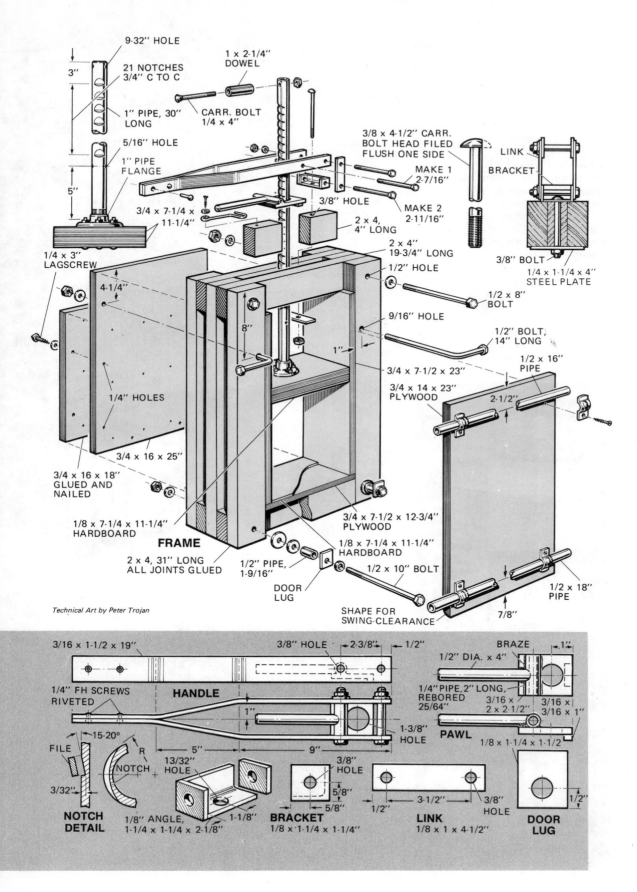

9-32" HOLE

3"

21 NOTCHES
3/4" C TO C

1 x 2-1/4"
DOWEL

1" PIPE, 30"
LONG

CARR. BOLT
1/4 x 4"

5/16" HOLE

3/8 x 4-1/2" CARR.
BOLT HEAD FILED
FLUSH ONE SIDE

LINK

1" PIPE
FLANGE

5"

BRACKET

MAKE 1
2-7/16"

3/4 x 7-1/4 x
11-1/4"

3/8" HOLE

MAKE 2
2-11/16"

3/8" BOLT

1/4 x 3"
LAGSCREW

2 x 4,
4" LONG

1/4 x 1-1/4 x 4"
STEEL PLATE

4-1/4"

2 x 4"
19-3/4" LONG

1/2" HOLE

8"

9/16" HOLE

1/2 x 8"
BOLT

1/4" HOLES

1"

3/4 x 7-1/2 x 23"

1/2 BOLT,
14" LONG

1/2 x 16"
PIPE

3/4 x 14 x 23"
PLYWOOD

3/4 x 16 x 25"

2-1/2"

3/4 x 16 x 18"
GLUED AND
NAILED

1/8 x 7-1/4 x 11-1/4"
HARDBOARD

FRAME

3/4 x 7-1/2 x 12-3/4"
PLYWOOD

2 x 4, 31" LONG
ALL JOINTS GLUED

1/2" PIPE,
1-9/16"

1/8 x 7-1/4 x 11-1/4"
HARDBOARD

DOOR
LUG

1/2 x 10" BOLT

1/2 x 18"
PIPE

SHAPE FOR
SWING-CLEARANCE

7/8"

Technical Art by Peter Trojan

3/16 x 1-1/2 x 19"

3/8" HOLE

2-3/8"

1/2"

BRAZE

1"

1/2" DIA. x 4"

1/4" FH SCREWS
RIVETED

HANDLE

1/4" PIPE, 2" LONG,
REBORED
25/64"

3/16 x
2 x 2-1/2"

3/16 x
3/16 x 1"

1"

1-3/8"
HOLE

PAWL

1/8 x 1-1/4 x 1-1/2

15-20°

FILE

R

5"

9"

3/8"
HOLE

3/32"

NOTCH

13/32"
HOLE

5/8"

NOTCH
DETAIL

1/8" ANGLE,
1-1/4 x 1-1/4 x 2-1/8"

1-1/8"

BRACKET
1/8 x 1-1/4 x 1-1/4"

5/8"

1/2"

LINK
1/8 x 1 x 4-1/2"

3-1/2"

3/8"
HOLE

DOOR
LUG

1/2"

Two views of the same unit show how this novel hi-fi center can change its appearance—and function—at the flick of a finger. Below, it shows off books, magazines, pictures and decorative objects—doesn't look at all like a housing for electronic gear. At right, swung around to its opposite side, it suddenly sports a speaker, tape deck, AM/FM stereo receiver, telephone and other equipment, ready for immediate use. At lower right is a mouth-watering setup for serving party snacks from a Panasonic electric fondue cooker on a slide-out shelf

Build a swivel hi-fi center

BY SHELDON M. GALLAGER

Turning on ball-bearing pivots, these stacking units can
hide home entertainment equipment when it's not in use
and swing it quickly into view for instant party fun

■ A SMART PIECE of furniture by day, an active entertainment center at night—that's the quick-change convenience you get from these stacking enclosures on rotating swivels. Each unit is designed to house one type of equipment on one side and another on the opposite side. Each swings freely on its own pivot, independently of the others. Turned one way, the units provide spaces for books, knick-knacks, pictures and other decorative objects. Swung the other way, the stack changes magically into a hi-fi center with speaker, tape deck, tuner, amplifier, record changer, television set and other electronic gear.

The units are simple boxes—in most cases, open at both ends—so there's no complicated carpentry involved. Three basic modular sizes can be combined in any order and number you wish to handle the particular equipment you have. All have an inside width of 19 inches with a choice of three heights—10½, 14 and 17½ inches. If you like to rack-mount your hi-fi components, you'll note that these dimensions correspond exactly to standard rack-panel sizes—another feature of the modular design. The shallowest unit is handy for small bookshelf-type speakers, receivers, amplifiers and similar low equipment. The middle-sized 14-inch module handles taller items such as a vertically mounted

A slide-out shelf is a versatile accessory that can make normally hard-to-reach equipment easily accessible. At the top, it holds a Garrard record changer; at the center, a Panasonic cassette tape deck; at the bottom, a Kodak Carousel slide projector. On the facing page, it doubles as a handy snack server for party guests, sporting one of Panasonic's colorful fondue cookers. The shelf is easy to make using standard 18-inch roller-bearing drawer slides available at hardware stores. A front lip and recessed side rails hide most of the hardware from view. One helpful hint: The rear edges of the shelf must be notched out so you can press down on the release catches to disengage the rails and remove the unit from the cabinet. Otherwise, the shelf will remain locked in once it is inserted

tape deck, table-model television set or record storage. The still larger 17½-inch unit provides extra overhead clearance for record players with swing-up covers and compact receivers with a turntable on top.

The column shown here is made up of five modules—one 10½-inch size at the top for a speaker, three 14-inchers for general use and one 17½-incher for bulky gear. Their total height comes to 82 inches—just short of 7 feet and about maximum for good appearance in an 8-foot room. All modules are square so they automatically line up with each other no matter

which way they're turned. Only the bottom unit doesn't rotate. This rests on a recessed kickboard and forms a fixed, stable base for the swiveling units above it.

All sorts of variations are possible, depending on the particular features you want. You'll note that one unit incorporates a colorful telephone niche, another a sloping magazine rack. The large unit houses a slide-out shelf, handy for quick access to equipment that needs to be reached from the top, such as a turntable, cassette tape deck or slide projector. The shelf can even be used as a mini pull-out bar or snack server for party fun. Internal partitions can be installed wherever needed to divide the units into double-sided enclosures open at either end. The top unit, for instance, houses a speaker on one

Swivel action permits the TV set to be turned for the best viewing angle, along with the speaker unit at the top. When not in use, the TV can be hidden from view. The light fixture is one of many dress-up touches

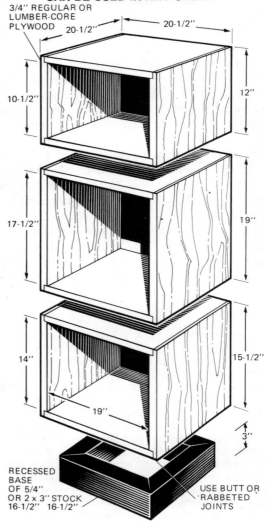

3 BASIC SIZES OF STACKING CABINETS CAN BE USED IN ANY ORDER

3/4" REGULAR OR LUMBER-CORE PLYWOOD

20-1/2"   20-1/2"

10-1/2"   12"

17-1/2"   19"

14"   15-1/2"

19"

3"

RECESSED BASE OF 5/4" OR 2 x 3" STOCK
16-1/2"   16-1/2"

USE BUTT OR RABBETED JOINTS

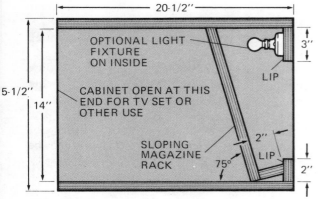

20-1/2"

OPTIONAL LIGHT
FIXTURE
ON INSIDE

3"

LIP

5-1/2"

14"

CABINET OPEN AT THIS
END FOR TV SET OR
OTHER USE

SLOPING
MAGAZINE
RACK

75°

2"

LIP

2"

The magazine rack is detailed in the drawing above

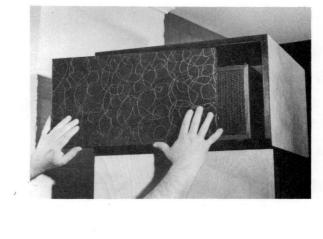

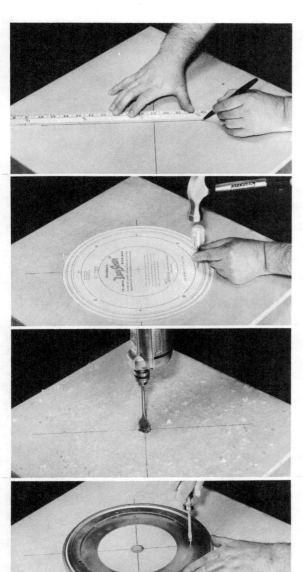

side, a shallow knickknack shelf on the other. The magazine rack hides a TV set in back; an innocent-appearing bookshelf conceals a reel-to-reel tape deck on the opposite side.

The swivels are standard 12-inch-diameter ballbearing types used for making lazy-Susan tables, rotating kitchen shelves and the like. They're available for about $4 each postpaid from Edmund Scientific Co., 300 Edscorp Building, Barrington, N.J. 08007. The swivels can support up to 1000 pounds apiece and turn with surprising ease, even when weighted with heavy hi-fi gear. Attaching them is easy because each comes with a cutout marking template to simplify the location of mounting screws. Power cords, speaker leads, audio cables and antenna wires run down through 1-inch-diameter center holes drilled in the top and bottom of each module. To avoid excessive twisting of the wires, simply remember not to turn the units constantly in the same direction. Rotate them one way to get at one side, then the other way to reach the opposite side.

Constructing the modules is easy because they fit so closely together (the swivels are only ⅜ inch thick) that corner joints are scarcely visible. You can use rabbeted joints if you wish, but simple butts will also do. The units shown here are made of ¾-inch solid-core birch plywood.

The swivels are easy to mount because they come with marking templates. At the top, the center is found by crisscrossing diagonals from the corners, then the template is used to mark screw holes with a hammer and punch. A center hole is drilled for the wires, then the swivel is screwed on (bottom photo). The photo at the top right shows a Heath speaker and slip-in grille of speaker cloth stapled to a 1 x 2 frame

Quick ways to spruce up the basement

Hide furnace, workshop,
 washer and dryer with quick-change
walls and screens; add some quick-made
 accessories, and that 'impossible'
basement will take on a party look with
 minimum effort and money. Then all you
 have to do is provide the entertainment

Party furniture that you can make yourself from inexpensive plywood can include these two clever card tables. The one above is a simple box with playing-card designs added to sides; table below is supported by a Lally column

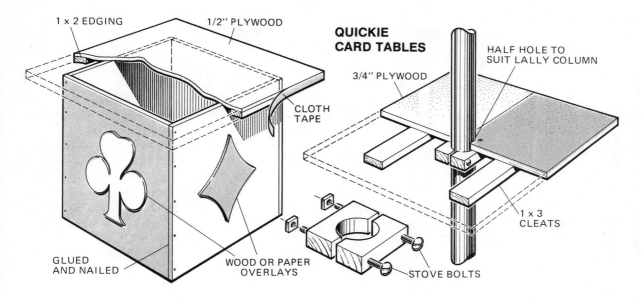

1 x 2 EDGING

1/2" PLYWOOD

QUICKIE
CARD TABLES

HALF HOLE TO
SUIT LALLY COLUMN

3/4" PLYWOOD

CLOTH
TAPE

1 x 3
CLEATS

GLUED
AND NAILED

WOOD OR PAPER
OVERLAYS

STOVE BOLTS

■ YOU'VE BEEN THINKING it would be fun to have a party—perhaps a big gang of 10 or more couples. But where will put them all? Your wife suggests the basement, if you fix it up a bit. But you shudder at the thought of trying to make it presentable without spending a bundle or a month of Sundays. You'll be surprised at what improvements you can accomplish for a few dollars and a minimum of effort.

Mostly, it's a case of "cover up"—hiding the furnace, oil tank, water heater; screening a washer and dryer from view, concealing your workshop or just covering up general basement clutter. Concealment alone covers a multitude of sins in sprucing up the most impossible basement.

There are other things you can do to give a party atmosphere to a dingy area. You can put Lally columns (the steel posts that support the

floor above) to work supporting home-built tables. You can slap a coat of quick-drying latex paint on drab concrete walls to brighten things up. You can solve a problem floor with a roll of gaily-striped indoor-outdoor carpeting. You can round up travel posters and photo blowups to help cover up and add a festive touch. And if you don't have the right kind of furniture, you can make it.

A typical small-home basement is shown below, and on this and the following four pages you'll find instructions for making the various cover-ups and accessories suggested.

LEGEND

1. Quickie card tables
2. Folding screen
3. Quick-change wall
4. Dummy louvered window
5. Game divider and screen
6. Decorative divider
7. Cube stools
8. Buffet table
9. Fuel-tank screen
10. Indoor-outdoor carpet

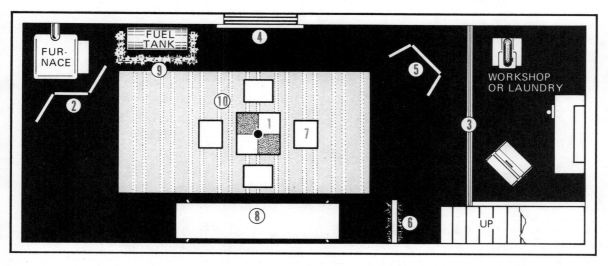

basement spruce-up, continued

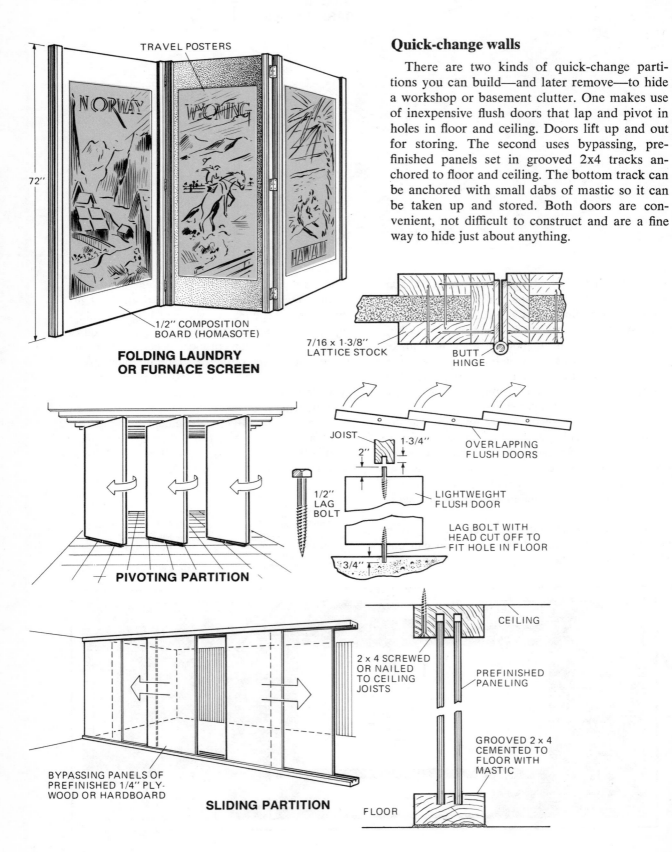

TRAVEL POSTERS

N O R W A Y

WYOMING

HAWAII

72"

1/2" COMPOSITION
BOARD (HOMASOTE)

**FOLDING LAUNDRY
OR FURNACE SCREEN**

Quick-change walls

There are two kinds of quick-change partitions you can build—and later remove—to hide a workshop or basement clutter. One makes use of inexpensive flush doors that lap and pivot in holes in floor and ceiling. Doors lift up and out for storing. The second uses bypassing, prefinished panels set in grooved 2x4 tracks anchored to floor and ceiling. The bottom track can be anchored with small dabs of mastic so it can be taken up and stored. Both doors are convenient, not difficult to construct and are a fine way to hide just about anything.

7/16 x 1-3/8"
LATTICE STOCK

BUTT
HINGE

OVERLAPPING
FLUSH DOORS

JOIST

2"

1-3/4"

1/2"
LAG
BOLT

LIGHTWEIGHT
FLUSH DOOR

LAG BOLT WITH
HEAD CUT OFF TO
FIT HOLE IN FLOOR

3/4"

PIVOTING PARTITION

CEILING

2 x 4 SCREWED
OR NAILED TO
CEILING
JOISTS

PREFINISHED
PANELING

GROOVED 2 x 4
CEMENTED TO
FLOOR WITH
MASTIC

BYPASSING PANELS OF
PREFINISHED 1/4" PLY-
WOOD OR HARDBOARD

SLIDING PARTITION

FLOOR

Dummy windows

For basement windows, curtains are the easy way out, but a more novel treatment uses narrow-louver shutters installed in dummy full-window frames. Attached to the wall, they take away the "basement look." If the upper shutters are hinged, the windows can be opened for ventilation.

Game dividers and screens

Folding game dividers such as a dartboard add fun to a party while hiding a washer and dryer or water heater. Legs grooved to fit plywood or hardboard are hinged to fold flat.

A conversation screen (lower right) also adds to an evening's fun when covered with humorous cartoons and pictures or posters. Its shelves provide handy places for those guests who always seem to need somewhere to set a drink or ashtray.

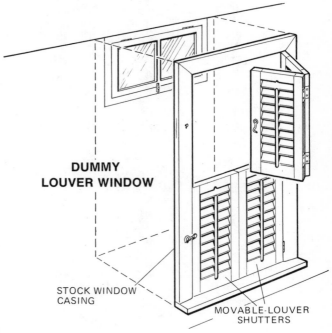

DUMMY LOUVER WINDOW

STOCK WINDOW CASING

MOVABLE-LOUVER SHUTTERS

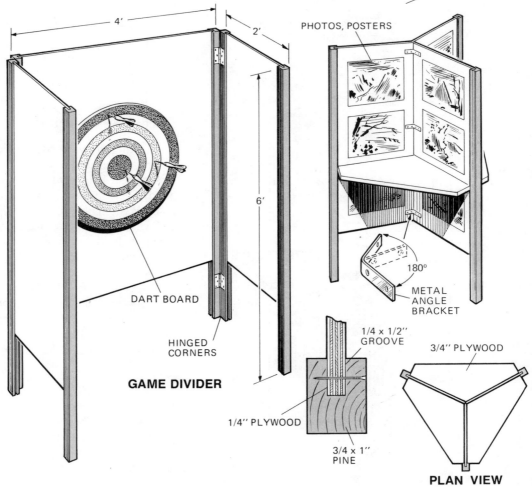

4'

2'

6'

DART BOARD

HINGED CORNERS

GAME DIVIDER

PHOTOS, POSTERS

180°

METAL ANGLE BRACKET

1/4 x 1/2" GROOVE

3/4" PLYWOOD

1/4" PLYWOOD

3/4 x 1" PINE

PLAN VIEW

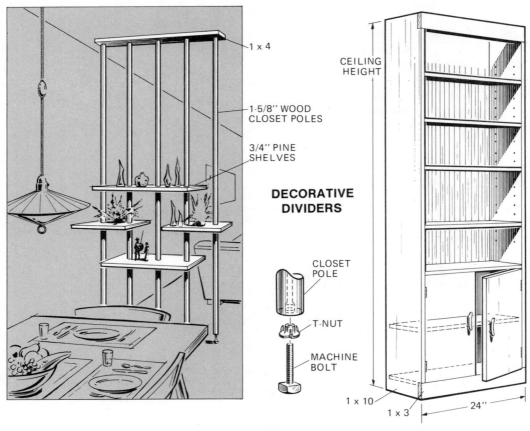

1 x 4

1-5/8" WOOD CLOSET POLES

3/4" PINE SHELVES

DECORATIVE DIVIDERS

CLOSET POLE

T-NUT

MACHINE BOLT

CEILING HEIGHT

1 x 10

1 x 3

24"

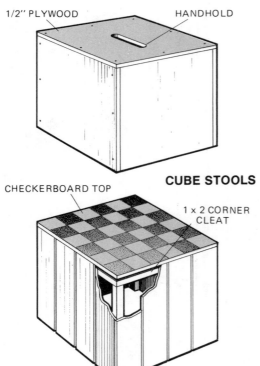

1/2" PLYWOOD

HANDHOLD

CUBE STOOLS

CHECKERBOARD TOP

1 x 2 CORNER CLEAT

Decorative dividers

Blocking the view of basement stairs or partitioning off an unwanted area with a ceiling-high divider will help spruce up a room and provide handy shelf space. The see-through one of closet poles is designed to wedge between floor and ceiling. Ends of poles are drilled for T-nuts and machine bolts. A wedging action is the result when the bolts are backed out to bear against the floor.

The bookcase divider offers shelves for a record player and hi-fi equipment, with album storage below. The whole thing is made from pine in standard lumberyard sizes, the back being a piece of prefinished paneling.

Cube stools

When chairs run out, cube stools help provide extra seating. They can also double as sit-on-the-floor game tables when the tops are checkerboards. They're just plywood boxes, for the most part, wildly painted in red, blue and yellow to add a gay party look to the occasion.

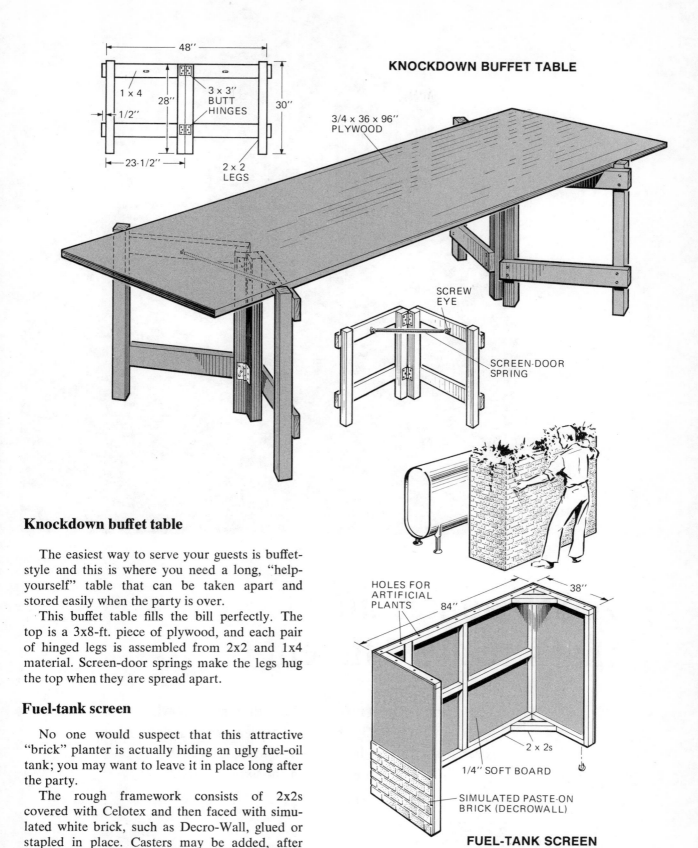

KNOCKDOWN BUFFET TABLE

48″

1 x 4

28″ 3 x 3″ BUTT HINGES

1/2″

30″

23-1/2″

2 x 2 LEGS

3/4 x 36 x 96″ PLYWOOD

SCREW EYE

SCREEN-DOOR SPRING

HOLES FOR ARTIFICIAL PLANTS

84″

38″

2 x 2s

1/4″ SOFT BOARD

SIMULATED PASTE-ON BRICK (DECROWALL)

FUEL-TANK SCREEN

Knockdown buffet table

The easiest way to serve your guests is buffet-style and this is where you need a long, "help-yourself" table that can be taken apart and stored easily when the party is over.

This buffet table fills the bill perfectly. The top is a 3x8-ft. piece of plywood, and each pair of hinged legs is assembled from 2x2 and 1x4 material. Screen-door springs make the legs hug the top when they are spread apart.

Fuel-tank screen

No one would suspect that this attractive "brick" planter is actually hiding an ugly fuel-oil tank; you may want to leave it in place long after the party.

The rough framework consists of 2x2s covered with Celotex and then faced with simulated white brick, such as Decro-Wall, glued or stapled in place. Casters may be added, after which some artificial greenery is stuck in the holes around the top to create the planter effect.

A $50 aquarium that's really different

This 'bubble' pond may at first resemble a huge salad bowl,
but when it's filled with water, fish and plants it
becomes a thing of beauty. Any handyman can make
this conversation piece for the living room

BY RONALD KONIECZYNSKI

■ YOU CAN BUY a conventional 30-gal. fish tank with stand for about what it will cost to build this beauty, but that's what you'll have—a conventional-looking aquarium.

Not so with this bubble pond. It's as different and unconventional as you'll find. Resembling a king-size salad bowl, it consists of a 30-in. diameter plastic bubble you buy and cradle in a simple half-lapped stand. When viewed from certain angles, the curved sides of the bubble magnify and produce weird and unusual effects that are fascinating to watch while the fish are swimming around a cascading waterfall.

The bubble comes with the edge trimmed and partially sanded so that it requires final finishing with fine sandpaper (150-grit followed by 220-grit) wrapped around a wood block. A sturdy cardboard box, about 18 in. square with the open end up and covered with a soft throw rug, makes a good marproof holder for your bubble while you work on it.

To get a professional-looking frosted finish on the lip, your sanding strokes should follow the curve of the bubble's rim. Your arm will sweep in a natural arc if you reach over the bubble and sand the far edge from the inside. Sand lightly and rapidly, changing sandpaper frequently. This job should take no more than 30 minutes.

When you are satisfied with the finish, break the sharp corners on both the inside and outside edges of the lip by rubbing them lightly with the sanding block held at a 45° angle. Then rinse away any grit by flushing the area with water and by swabbing it lightly with a wet sponge. Your bubble is now ready for mounting on a stand.

I made the stand of 5/4 x 10-in. premium-quality redwood and later finished it to look like walnut. The two legs of the stand are identical except for the interlapping notches. Lay out the pattern for the legs on cardboard, making the curve match the bubble. Nominally, this curve will be the same as the diameter of the bubble (15-in. radius) so you can use the bubble's lip to trace the curve on your cardboard.

After you cut out the template, check it to see how well it fits the bubble. While a perfect fit is

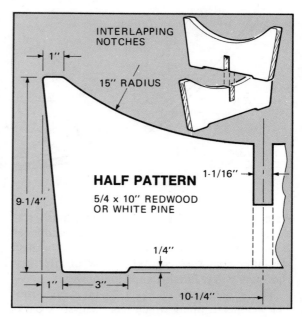

INTERLAPPING NOTCHES

15" RADIUS

HALF PATTERN
5/4 x 10" REDWOOD
OR WHITE PINE

1"

9-1/4"

1-1/16"

1/4"

1"   3"

10-1/4"

not critical, there should be no more than a $\frac{1}{16}$-in. gap at any point.

Next, trace the pattern for both legs on the wood; saw out and round all edges and corners before cutting the notches. The notches are formed by making two straight saw cuts and breaking out the wood between with a chisel. After notching, finish-sand the flat faces prior to assembly. Notching is done most accurately on a table saw, running up the blade as high as possible and feeding the work with the saw's miter gauge. Two parallel saw cuts will result in both members of the cradle. However, you must remember to stop the cut short of its mark on the top side of the work to allow for the curvature of the blade which makes a deeper cut on the underside of the work. A handsaw is used to finish and even up the cuts.

If the notches are a snug fit, you won't need glue—simply slide one into the other. If the notches happen to fit loosely, use some resorcinol resin glue to help fill the gaps and strengthen the joint. Wipe off any excess glue right away with a slightly damp rag.

Fruitwood oil stain produces a handsome walnut finish when applied to redwood. After the

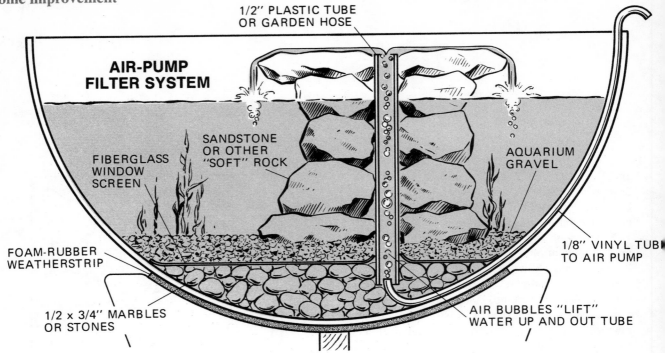

AIR-PUMP FILTER SYSTEM

1/2" PLASTIC TUBE OR GARDEN HOSE

FIBERGLASS WINDOW SCREEN

SANDSTONE OR OTHER "SOFT" ROCK

AQUARIUM GRAVEL

1/8" VINYL TUBE TO AIR PUMP

FOAM-RUBBER WEATHERSTRIP

1/2 x 3/4" MARBLES OR STONES

AIR BUBBLES "LIFT" WATER UP AND OUT TUBE

stain is dry, apply three coats of satin-finish urethane varnish. Sand lightly with fine sandpaper between the second and third coats and burnish the latter coat with No. 00 steel wool after it is thoroughly dry. Finally, apply paste wax.

The bubble rests on $\frac{5}{16}$ x $\frac{3}{4}$-in. sponge-rubber weatherstripping which has a self-stick backing. The self-stick side is placed up and its protective paper covering is left intact while the strip is cemented to the stand. Coat the strip with contact cement and press it in place while the

cement is still tacky. This will give you time to shift the strip when centering it.

While the rubber strips are drying, you can go ahead and mount the bubble. The rim of the bubble must be parallel to the base of the stand because any slant will be obvious when the bubble is filled with water.

First, set the bubble in its wooden cradle on the floor where it will be used and shift its position until a level placed across the rim shows it to be level. Now mark the position of the bubble

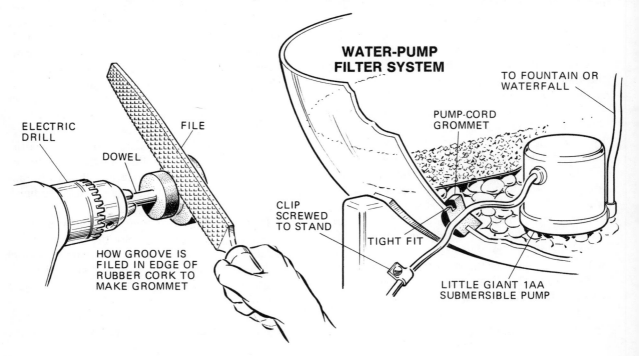

ELECTRIC DRILL

FILE

DOWEL

HOW GROOVE IS FILED IN EDGE OF RUBBER CORK TO MAKE GROMMET

WATER-PUMP FILTER SYSTEM

TO FOUNTAIN OR WATERFALL

PUMP-CORD GROMMET

CLIP SCREWED TO STAND

TIGHT FIT

LITTLE GIANT 1AA SUBMERSIBLE PUMP

with respect to the cradle by sticking pieces of masking tape on the inside and in line with the legs. Lift the bubble, remove the protective paper from the weatherstripping and place the plastic shell back in the cradle as it was. Finally, fill the bubble with water to weight it and bring it firmly against the sticky strips.

You have a choice of two filter systems. One employs an air pump located outside the bubble; the other a submersible water pump placed in the middle of the bubble. Each system has its advantages; the clear vinyl tubing used with the air pump is inconspicuous and doesn't need hiding, whereas the electric cord to the water pump is not easily concealed and requires running it out a hole in the bottom of the bubble. Boring a hole in the plastic for a watertight grommet is not difficult if you use a saw-type hole cutter in a slow-speed drill and exert only light pressure.

The drawings show two ways of creating planter islands in the center of your bubble.

The cascade planter consists of a tier of plastic flowerpots joined by a threaded rod. The lower end of the rod is attached to a plastic disc, which in turn is weighted with stones and aquarium gravel. Here water bubbles up through the stones in the top pot and cascades from pot to pot.

plants rooted in soil

The arrowhead plants in the two lower pots are rooted in soil that is covered by a layer of stones to keep the dirt from washing out. The vine in the top pot is bedded directly in the stones without dirt and thrives on the continuously circulating water. Discs of plastic or hardboard are placed inside and under each pot and used to clamp the pots to the threaded rod with nuts and washers. The tubing from the filter pump is snaked up through holes in pots and the discs. A disc of fiberglass window screen in the top pot deflects the water and prevents it from dislodging the stones.

When filled with water, your bubble pond will weigh up to 300 lbs. so decide on a permanent location before you fill it. Moving it afterward would surely be difficult.

Follow the usual rules in maintaining an aquarium: Avoid overstocking with fish and overfeeding. A couple dozen small goldfish and a dime-store turtle or two make a fine beginning. Turtles need a rock or two to climb onto.

You can order a 30-in. plastic bubble from E. F. P. Products, Box 8243, North Royalton, Ohio 44133. It is priced at about $35 plus shipping.

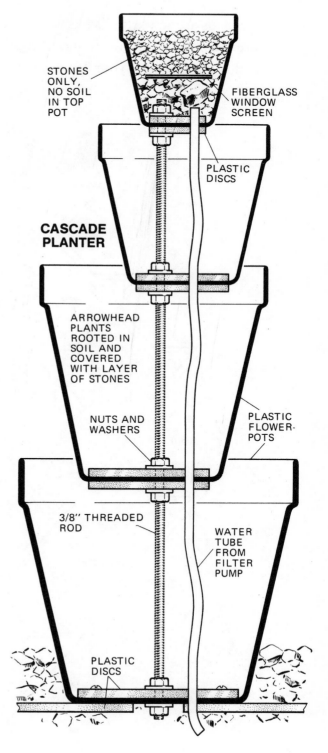

STONES ONLY, NO SOIL IN TOP POT

FIBERGLASS WINDOW SCREEN

PLASTIC DISCS

CASCADE PLANTER

ARROWHEAD PLANTS ROOTED IN SOIL AND COVERED WITH LAYER OF STONES

NUTS AND WASHERS

PLASTIC FLOWER-POTS

3/8" THREADED ROD

WATER TUBE FROM FILTER PUMP

PLASTIC DISCS

A flower garden on the wall

This attractive trellis lets you move a bit
of nature indoors. It's just the thing to brighten
up that blank wall in your den or living room

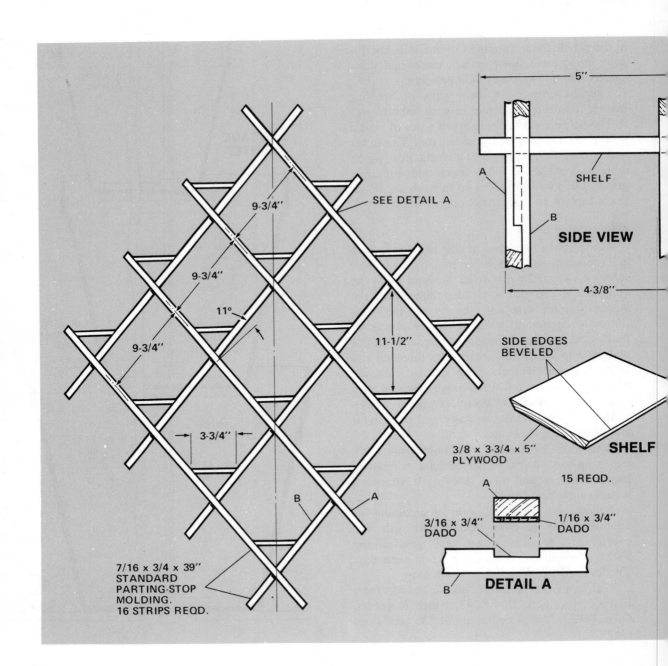

SEE DETAIL A

9-3/4"

9-3/4"

11°

9-3/4"

11-1/2"

3-3/4"

B

A

7/16 x 3/4 x 39"
STANDARD
PARTING-STOP
MOLDING.
16 STRIPS REQD.

5"

SHELF

A

B

SIDE VIEW

4-3/8"

SIDE EDGES
BEVELED

3/8 x 3-3/4 x 5"
PLYWOOD

SHELF

15 REQD.

A

3/16 x 3/4"
DADO

1/16 x 3/4"
DADO

B

DETAIL A

THIS COLORFUL PLANT TRELLIS is a decoration that literally "grows" on the wall. Fifteen potted plants give it an ever-changing look as new foliage and blossoms appear.

The trellis consists of two identical frames of crisscrossed strips spaced apart by 15 shelves. The strips are lumberyard moldings which measure approximately ½ x ¾ in. You'll need 16 strips (39 in. long)—8 dadoed 3/16 in. deep and 8 dadoed 1/16 in. deep to automatically register one strip over the other. The dadoes are cut with a table or radial saw, and with a stop attached to the fence to space the cuts uniformly 9¾ in. on centers. The blade, or the miter gauge, as the case may be, is set 11° left of 90°; the same setting is used in dadoing all 16 pieces. The ends of the shelves are beveled to suit and then the shelves are glued even with the front and back strips.

Finish the completed trellis with white paint. Shop around for some colorful pots and add the plants of your choice.

The white-painted trellis with its many different-colored pots contrasts beautifully when hung on a dark paneled wall (above). A couple of screws through holes in the back strips are used to hang the unit. The plastic pots are from a variety store. Shop around until you find some that are attractive and inexpensive

With the screen retracted (left), the unit looks like an ordinary wall cabinet with storage cupboards and knickknack shelves. Conversion to home theater (above) takes only seconds, makes showing slides or movies fun instead of a nuisance. The unit can be anchored to wall or suspended on shelf brackets

A hideaway home theater

BY SHELDON M. GALLAGER

■ BY THE TIME you haul out all the gear required to put on a slide or movie show, a lot of the fun has gone for you and your guests. This hideaway wall unit is designed to end the fuss and put the fun back into showing slides and movies. There's no screen to get out and set up because it's already built into the unit—you just pull it down and slip the projector out of one of the side cabinets.

When the screen is not in use, it disappears up into a recess at the top and is completely hidden from view. In its place are shelves for displaying decorative objects, giving the unit an attractive appearance when it's not serving as an instant home theater. The cabinets, besides storing photographic gear, can also house hi-fi equipment, making the unit an all-around home entertainment center. The cabinets are spaced apart just right for good stereo listening from small bookshelf-type speakers placed inside the cupboards. The doors have mesh-covered openings designed to let sound through.

If you go in for sound movies or sound-synced slide shows, the setup is ideal because the accompanying sound, filtering out through the mesh doors, will appear to come right from the projection screen. For added convenience, you can install one of NuTone's flush-mounting music/intercom systems, as shown in the photos below. These systems come in a variety of types and price ranges and offer a complete home communication center in a single, smartly styled unit with built-in radio, speaker and intercom controls.

The wall unit is built around a 40x40-inch pull-down screen made by Da-Lite. This type is designed expressly for wall or ceiling mounting and has brackets on the case that permit the screen to be hung from hooks or attached with screws. Such screens cost about the same as the regular floor-stand type.

Dimensions of the unit can be altered as desired, but the 10-inch depth was chosen because it enables all parts except the back panels to be ripped from stock 1x12-inch lumber with little waste. The unit can be screwed directly to the wall, just as you would mount a kitchen cabinet, or it can be supported on metal shelf brackets of the type that hook into slotted wall standards. The 10-inch depth enables the unit to fit perfectly on standard 10-inch-long shelf brackets.

If you decide on wall brackets, one construction pointer is important. The unit should be

Underside view with fascia board removed shows how the screen mounts at top of the unit between cabinets. With fascia board in place, the screen is hidden from view. Screen shown here is a 40 x 40-inch model made by Da-Lite. Two-way end brackets permit it to be hung from hooks or attached with screws

supported on no fewer than *three* brackets—one at each end and one at the middle. The center bracket can't extend the full cabinet depth, however, or it would obviously block the screen from coming down. The answer here is to build up a small supporting framework at the center of the span just behind the screen. This framework is 6 inches deep and rests on a 6-inch shelf bracket, supporting the middle of the unit without interfering with the operation of the screen. The knickknack shelves also rest on 6-inch brackets,

Hanging side cabinets can house various pieces of equipment depending on your needs. Here, one is fitted with NuTone's in-a-wall music/intercom system designed to mount in shallow spaces. Upper unit (left, below) is AM/FM radio with 10-station intercom. Lower unit is fold-up record changer that swings out horizontally for use (center). Opposite cabinet (right) holds a Kodak Super-8 movie projector, film reels and a Model AS-18 Heathkit speaker

providing sufficient clearance for the screen to pull down in front.

For maximum strength, the main strut running across the back at the top should extend the full 80-inch width—behind the cabinets as well as the screen—since it supports the entire weight of the unit where hung on shelf brackets. If you plan to mount the unit directly on the wall, you can, of course, eliminate the strut and center supporting framework.

Other options and variations are possible, too. As shown here, the unit incorporates a recess at the top for installing fluorescent lighting fixtures. These provide a soft, pleasing cove lighting effect. You can also build just the screen enclosure without the hanging side cabinets. Several alternate versions of this type are shown. Further information on screens can be obtained from Da-Lite Screen Co., Warsaw, Ind. 46580. For more details on Nu-Tone's in-a-wall music/intercom systems, write to NuTone Div., Madison and Red Bank Rds., Cincinnati, Ohio 45227.

home theater, continued

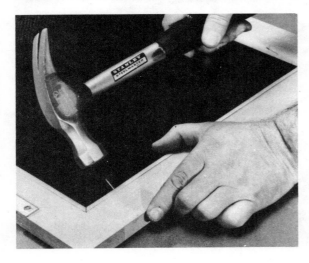

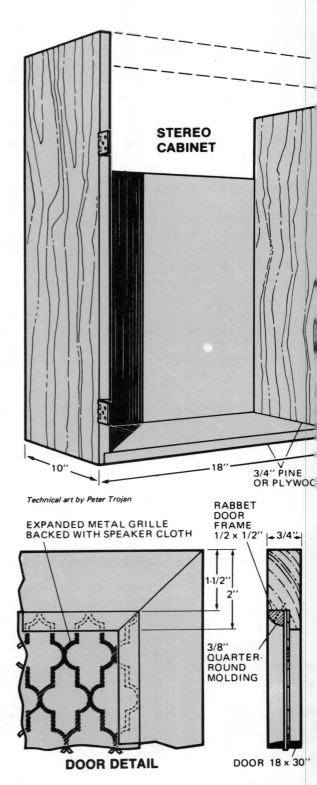

STEREO CABINET

10''   18''   3/4'' PINE OR PLYWOO

Technical art by Peter Trojan

EXPANDED METAL GRILLE BACKED WITH SPEAKER CLOTH

RABBET DOOR FRAME 1/2 x 1/2''   3/4''

1-1/2''

2''

3/8'' QUARTER-ROUND MOLDING

DOOR DETAIL

DOOR 18 x 30''

Grille-covered openings in doors are designed to let sound through even when the doors are closed. Door rails are rabbeted to form recess on back side, then decorative Reynolds brass mesh is trimmed with tin snips to fit inside (top photo at left). The mesh is backed with black speaker cloth, and both are held in place with ⅜-inch quarter-round molding strips tacked in with small brads

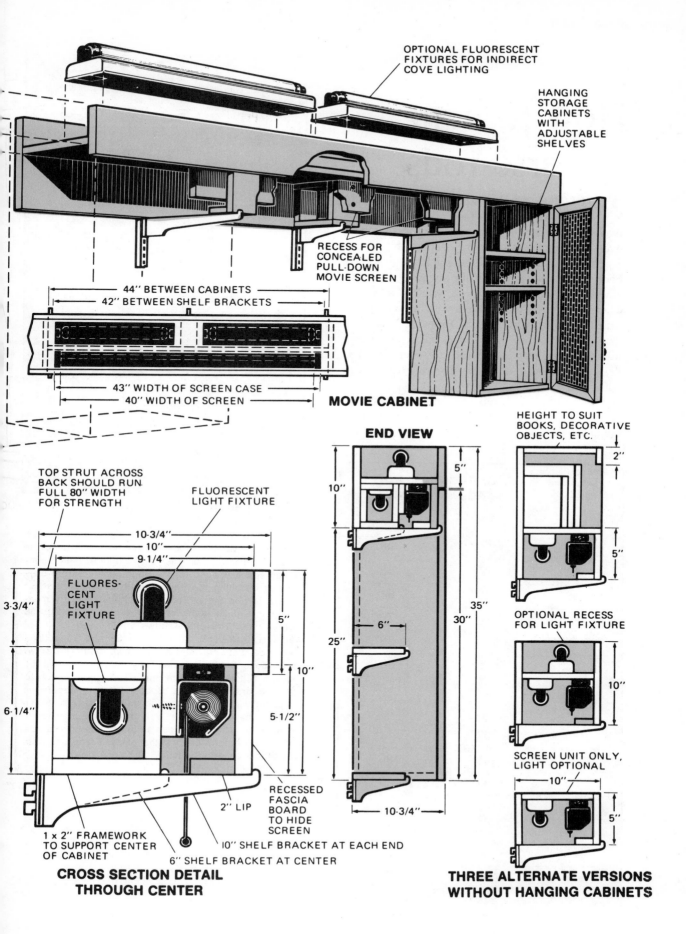

OPTIONAL FLUORESCENT FIXTURES FOR INDIRECT COVE LIGHTING

HANGING STORAGE CABINETS WITH ADJUSTABLE SHELVES

RECESS FOR CONCEALED PULL-DOWN MOVIE SCREEN

44'' BETWEEN CABINETS
42'' BETWEEN SHELF BRACKETS

43'' WIDTH OF SCREEN CASE
40'' WIDTH OF SCREEN

MOVIE CABINET

END VIEW

HEIGHT TO SUIT BOOKS, DECORATIVE OBJECTS, ETC.

2''

5''

OPTIONAL RECESS FOR LIGHT FIXTURE

10''

SCREEN UNIT ONLY, LIGHT OPTIONAL

10''

5''

TOP STRUT ACROSS BACK SHOULD RUN FULL 80'' WIDTH FOR STRENGTH

FLUORESCENT LIGHT FIXTURE

10-3/4''
10''
9-1/4''

3-3/4''

FLUORES-CENT LIGHT FIXTURE

5''

10''

6-1/4''

5-1/2''

2'' LIP

RECESSED FASCIA BOARD TO HIDE SCREEN

1 x 2'' FRAMEWORK TO SUPPORT CENTER OF CABINET

10'' SHELF BRACKET AT EACH END

6'' SHELF BRACKET AT CENTER

CROSS SECTION DETAIL THROUGH CENTER

5''
10''
6''
25''
30''
35''
10-3/4''

THREE ALTERNATE VERSIONS WITHOUT HANGING CABINETS

How to hang traverse rods

■ PUTTING UP new drapery rods so they stay is a job all homeowners face at times, whether they're moving into a new home or switching over to today's bold, new drapery hardware. Since the popular trend is to stack the draperies back off the glass, you won't always find a stud where you want it. If you do, you're lucky, but chances are you'll be faced with attaching the brackets to a hollow part of the wall. You can't drive plain screws into the plaster; they won't hold. The answer is a Molly fastener which is designed to hold anything securely to a wall without a stud.

Plan to place brackets for the rods above the casing, or at least 4 in. above the glass and an equal distance from the ceiling.

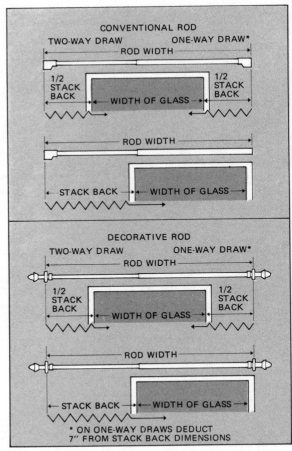

How to find the right rod length

With a draw treatment, it's best to have the draperies stack back over the window frame and wall, uncovering all the glass. To do this you must know the amount of wall space needed for the open panels before buying and installing the traverse rods. Use the chart at the left to find the correct rod length. Begin by measuring the glass width of your window. Say it's 38 inches wide. The chart shows you'll need 26 in. of wall for stack-back. So you add 38 and 26 in. and you'll see that you need a rod 64 in. long. The drawings above illustrate where the stack-back will be located. Stack-back is the amount of space occupied by open draw draperies. Space will vary depending on panel width, pleat spacing and fabric bulk. Since windows have two sides, you divide the stack-back distance in half (in this case 13 in.) to see how far the rod should extend beyond the glass. If you use one-way draperies, add the full 26 in. to one side

GLASS WIDTH	STACKBACK SPACE	ROD WIDTH
20″	20″	40″
26″	22″	48″
32″	24″	56″
38″	26″	64″
44″	28″	72″
50″	30″	80″
56″	32″	88″
62″	34″	96″
68″	36″	104″
75″	37″	112″
81″	39″	120″
87″	41″	128″
94″	42″	136″
100″	44″	144″
106″	46″	152″
112″	48″	160″
119″	49″	168″

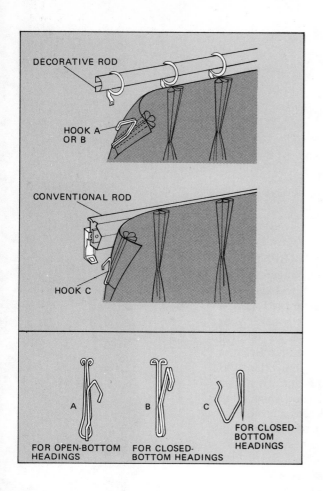

Selecting proper drapery hooks

The right drapery hooks can mean the difference between tip-tilt headings and those that stand properly erect. Always important, your choice of hooks is vital to the proper appearance of draperies hung on decorative traverse rods. At each window you will need one hook for each drapery pleat, plus four for returns and overlaps. On a decorative rod, the heading covers the pendants and falls just below the bottom of the rings. On a conventional rod, the heading extends to cover the rod. Thus hooks for conventional rods must be longer from the top of the hook to the top of the shank than hooks used for decorative rods

Ways to anchor brackets securely

Correct fastening devices are a must for proper installation of drapery hardware. Wood screws 1¼ in. long threaded the full length of the shanks are suitable for attaching brackets to studs. If wood studs can't be located or bracket-location falls between studs, Mollies (hollow-wall anchors) should be used as shown below. They are inserted in holes drilled through plaster or dry wall, tapped flush with the surface to embed the points and finally pulled up tight on the back by turning the screw that comes with the anchor. When mounting the modern, lightweight drapery rods on the wall, you can use plastic screw anchors. These easy-to-use tapered sleeve-type plugs are tapped in place in undersize holes drilled right through the plaster. Then simply find a full-thread wood screw of the proper size and turn it into the plug. As you turn it in, it spreads the split plastic sleeve and anchors it securely in place

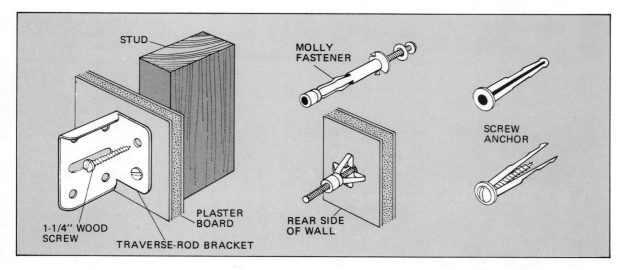

Workshop fit for a pro

BY HARRY WICKS

This workbench was first built back in 1951.
We've updated it with some new ideas and materials

■ A WELL-PLANNED WORKBENCH is what a good shop is all about, regardless of whether you are fortunate enough to have more than enough space or are shoehorned into a small work area. The bench is where your projects—big and little—will start, be labored over and, in all probability, be finished. Because a poor bench can easily diminish your interest as well as craftsmanship, use foresight when you build. Know what comprises a good shop setup and, if necessary, vary details and dimensions so they suit your own needs and preferences. Con-

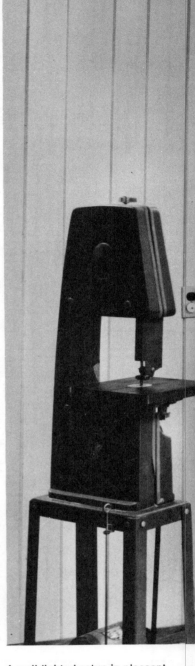

A well-lighted setup in pleasant surroundings makes work a pleasure. The end vise and bench boardstops let the user keep both hands on power tools where they belong. A roomy wall cabinet (above left) is pretty much the way it was shown 20 years ago except that the rails, stiles, doors and drawer fronts are covered with plastic laminate. The sturdy workbench boasts two vises, three roomy drawers and good-size shelves for portable power-tool storage. The kickplate is also a new feature

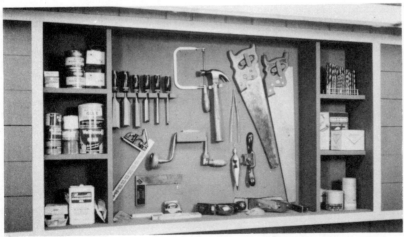

sidered by most experts to be the heart of the shop, a good workbench will include:

• A spacious, smooth work surface atop a sturdy and rigid base.

• At least one woodworking vise.

• Maximum small-parts and tool storage.

Because the approach here to building a workbench has been total—a setup rather than a workbench alone—you'll see more features than the three points just mentioned, including:

• A smooth top of more than 1100 sq. in., with an 8-in.-wide shaving trough.

• Two vises, provisions for bench dogs in the top and dowel supports in the apron to support long, vise-held workpieces.

• Storage galore. The base has three roomy, compartmentalized drawers and three shelves for portable-tool storage. Each end is finished with perforated board for extra tool hanging. The wall cabinet has 12 drawers, 6 shelves and a tool panel for fingertip convenience. There's also an overhead shop-built light fixture, a kickplate between bench feet to prevent dropped tools from rolling under the bench and plastic laminate on all exposed surfaces to minimize maintenance.

With minimum upkeep in mind, cabinet, bench and drawer interiors were left natural, merely varnished to make less obvious those inevitable smudge marks from tools and hands. Johns-Manville Melamite plastic laminate was used on exposed surfaces; marks and dirt will sponge off.

The bench, cabinet and light fixture were built

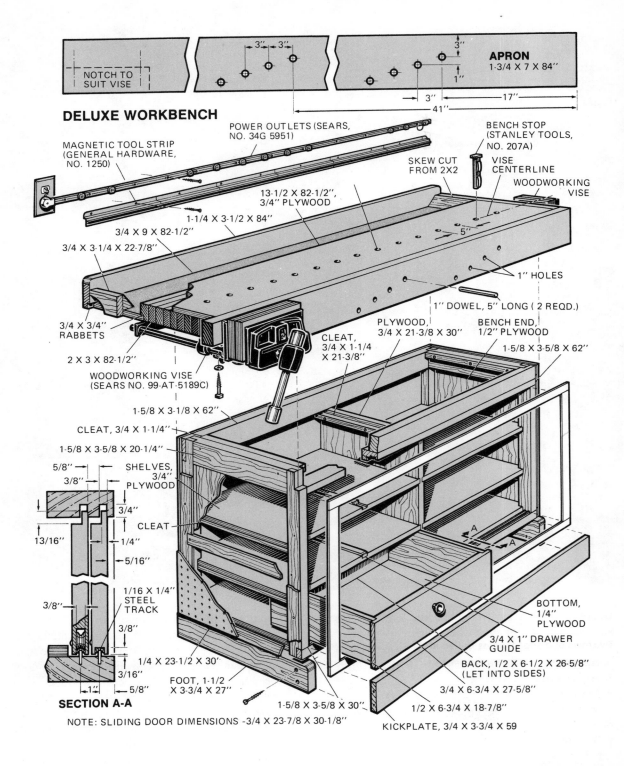

DELUXE WORKBENCH

APRON
1-3/4 X 7 X 84"

NOTCH TO SUIT VISE

MAGNETIC TOOL STRIP (GENERAL HARDWARE, NO. 1250)

POWER OUTLETS (SEARS, NO. 34G 5951)

BENCH STOP (STANLEY TOOLS, NO. 207A)

SKEW CUT FROM 2X2

VISE CENTERLINE

WOODWORKING VISE

13-1/2 X 82-1/2", 3/4" PLYWOOD

1-1/4 X 3-1/2 X 84"

3/4 X 9 X 82-1/2"

3/4 X 3-1/4 X 22-7/8"

1" HOLES

1" DOWEL, 5" LONG (2 REQD.)

3/4 X 3/4" RABBETS

2 X 3 X 82-1/2"

WOODWORKING VISE (SEARS NO. 99-AT-5189C)

PLYWOOD, 3/4 X 21-3/8 X 30"

CLEAT, 3/4 X 1-1/4 X 21-3/8"

BENCH END, 1/2" PLYWOOD

1-5/8 X 3-5/8 X 62"

1-5/8 X 3-1/8 X 62"

CLEAT, 3/4 X 1-1/4"

1-5/8 X 3-5/8 X 20-1/4"

SHELVES, 3/4" PLYWOOD

CLEAT

1/16 X 1/4" STEEL TRACK

1/4 X 23-1/2 X 30"

FOOT, 1-1/2 X 3-3/4 X 27"

1-5/8 X 3-5/8 X 30"

BOTTOM, 1/4" PLYWOOD

3/4 X 1" DRAWER GUIDE

BACK, 1/2 X 6-1/2 X 26-5/8" (LET INTO SIDES)

3/4 X 6-3/4 X 27-5/8"

1/2 X 6-3/4 X 18-7/8"

KICKPLATE, 3/4 X 3-3/4 X 59

SECTION A-A

NOTE: SLIDING DOOR DIMENSIONS -3/4 X 23-7/8 X 30-1/8"

from stock lumberyard items. For parts you may have to order, such as plexiglass and board stops, check the source list on page 102.

Sliding doors of the bench ride sheaves that roll on steel tracks that parallel the full length of the bottom front rail. Each door is fitted with

two sheaves set in 2 in. from the ends. Its top edge is rabbeted to engage grooves along the underside of the top rail. The ¾-in.-deep grooves allow ample clearance to place sheaves on the tracks when you install the doors. If you wish, you could alter dimensions and install com-

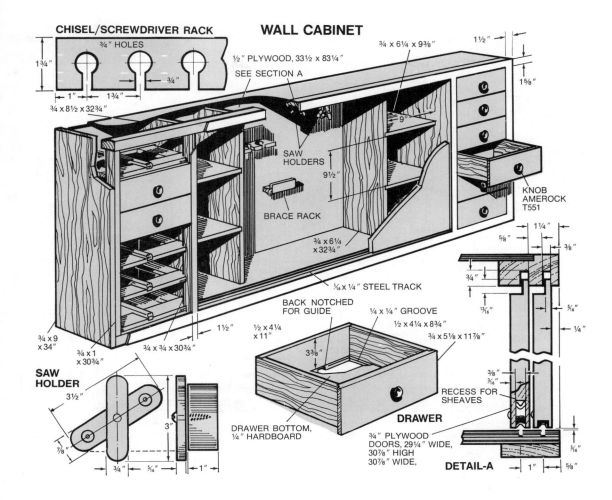

CHISEL/SCREWDRIVER RACK

3/4" HOLES
1 3/4"
1" 1 3/4"
3/4"
3/4 x 8 1/2 x 32 3/4"

WALL CABINET

1/2" PLYWOOD, 33 1/2 x 83 1/4"
SEE SECTION A

3/4 x 6 1/4 x 9 3/8"
1 1/2"
1 5/8"

9"

SAW HOLDERS
9 1/2"

BRACE RACK

KNOB AMEROCK T551

3/4 x 6 1/4 x 32 3/4"

1/16 x 1/4" STEEL TRACK

1 1/4"
5/8"
3/8"
3/4"
13/16"
5/16"
1/4"

3/4 x 9 x 34"
3/4 x 1 x 30 3/4"
3/4 x 3/4 x 30 3/4"
1 1/2"

BACK NOTCHED FOR GUIDE

1/4 x 1/4" GROOVE
1/2 x 4 1/4 x 8 3/4"
3/4 x 5 1/8 x 11 7/8"

1/2 x 4 1/4 x 11"
3 3/8"

3/8"
3/16"
RECESS FOR SHEAVES

SAW HOLDER

3 1/2"
3"
7/8"
3/4" 5/16" 1"

DRAWER BOTTOM, 1/4" HARDBOARD

DRAWER

3/4" PLYWOOD DOORS, 29 1/4" WIDE, 30 7/8" HIGH 30 7/8" WIDE,

3/8"
3/16"
3/16"

DETAIL-A
1" 5/8"

mercially available sliding-door hardware packaged in kits. But don't skimp on quality; these doors will get considerable hard use.

The original design of the workbench and wall cabinet had square holes in the benchtop. We've replaced these with 5/8-in.-dia. holes for use with

bench board stops. You may not find these stops readily at hardware stores but they can be ordered through your local hardware dealer. Essentially, they are industrial-school-shop items.

Unused space at the ends of the bench made little sense so we furred both ends and covered

Both workbench ends are furred and covered with perforated board for extra tool stoage. Two rows of diagonal holes drilled in the bench apron receive 1-in. dowels for supporting   long boards

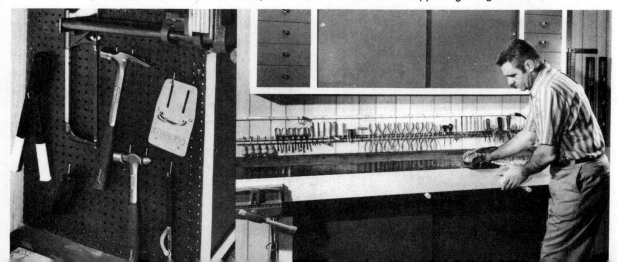

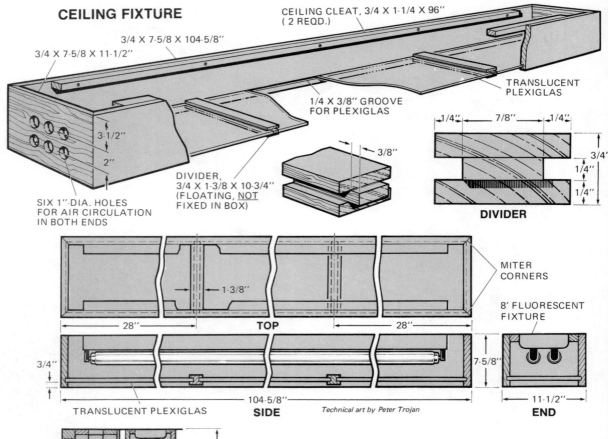

CEILING FIXTURE

CEILING CLEAT, 3/4 X 1-1/4 X 96"
(2 REQD.)

3/4 X 7-5/8 X 104-5/8"

3/4 X 7-5/8 X 11-1/2"

TRANSLUCENT
PLEXIGLAS

1/4 X 3/8" GROOVE
FOR PLEXIGLAS

3-1/2"

2"

3/8"

1/4"   7/8"   1/4"

3/4"
1/4"
1/4"

SIX 1"-DIA. HOLES
FOR AIR CIRCULATION
IN BOTH ENDS

DIVIDER,
3/4 X 1-3/8 X 10-3/4"
(FLOATING, NOT
FIXED IN BOX)

DIVIDER

1-3/8"

MITER
CORNERS

8' FLUORESCENT
FIXTURE

28"

TOP

28"

3/4"

7-5/8"

TRANSLUCENT PLEXIGLAS

104-5/8"

SIDE

Technical art by Peter Trojan

11-1/2"

END

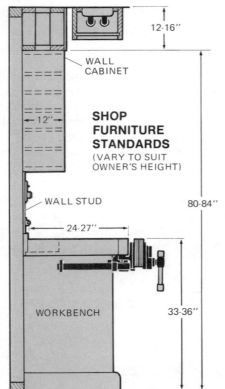

12-16"

WALL
CABINET

**SHOP
FURNITURE
STANDARDS**
(VARY TO SUIT
OWNER'S HEIGHT)

12"

WALL STUD

24-27"

80-84"

WORKBENCH

33-36"

them with perforated board. After applying two coats of semigloss varnish, we used the boards to hold tools and supplies that are needed infrequently. The fixture shown on page 99 was purchased without a hood and fastened directly to the ceiling. The surrounding box of 1x8 pine was grooved to receive removable plexiglass panels. The wood was simply stained and given two coats of semigloss varnish.

Consider adding a power outlet strip and magnetic toolholders to the wall between bench and cabinet. You can plug in several tools while you work on a project without having to switch power back and forth, and the holders keep your frequently used tools at hand in full view.

SPECIALTY ITEMS USED IN CONSTRUCTION
Drawer knobs, Amerock Corp., Rockford Ill. *No. T551*
Board stops, Stanley Tools, New Britain, Conn. *No. 207A*
Power outlets, Sears, Roebuck and Co. *Cat. No. 34G 5951*
Magnetic tool strip, General Hardware, 80 White St.,
   New York, N.Y. 10013. *No. 1250*
Plastic laminate, Johns-Manville, 300 Canal St., Lawrence,
   Mass. 01840. *Melamite*
Woodworking vise, Sears. *Cat. No. 99-AT-5189C*
Sheet acrylics (light fixture), Rohm & Haas, Box 9730,
   Philadelphia, Pa. 19140. *Translucent Plexiglas*
Walls, Masonite Corp., 29 North Wacker Dr., Chicago, Ill.
   60606. *Georgetown White 1900*

■ HERE'S A PROJECT you can finish in an evening—an extension-cord reel that plays out as much line as you need, when you need it. Mounted on a swivel bearing, the cord unwinds quickly; when you're through with it, you merely crank it up.

It goes together quickly. Use two small screws through predrilled ³⁄₁₆-in. holes to attach the utility box to the plywood disc. Run the cord through two Romex connectors, one installed on the side of the can and the other in a knockout of the utility box. Leave about 8 in. of cord protruding from the box, then mount it using two round-head screws in the drilled holes. The disc with a rectangular cutout can now be installed with screws. Mount the swivel bearing on the upright first, then to the reel. To maintain polarity, wire the outlet as shown in the drawing.

Extension-cord reel

You can avoid those annoying tangles in your extension cord with this easy-to-make windup reel

BY JOHN CAPOTOSTO

Two-lb. coffee can is the reel core

The cord reel can be assembled in one evening for pennies—the electric box and duplex will probably be your only expenses. When a job is finished, the cord is quickly cranked onto the reel

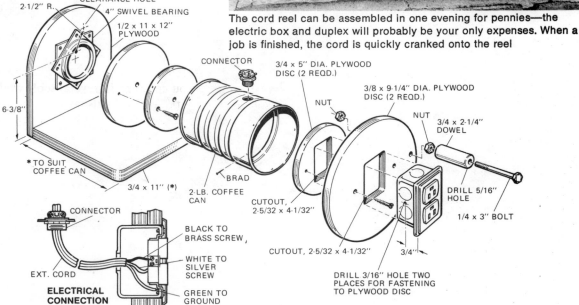

For versatility you can't beat a sabre saw

■ AS JIGSAWS, sabre saws aren't really very satisfactory. But as general-purpose power saws for cutting off lumber and ripping panel stock— the kinds of jobs that used to be done with arm-powered handsaws—the tools just can't be beat. Although sabre saws aren't as fast cutting as portable circular saws, they're lighter, easier to handle, safer and more versatile.

Their versatility has made them so popular,

particularly with homeowners who don't have table or radial saws, that there are now more than 20 makes of sabre saws available, and most manufacturers offer several different models—in all, a good many saws to choose from.

All are similar mechanically. In each a brush-type, universal motor pinion-drives a reduction gear that has an eccentric stud. The stud operates a reciprocating saw bar with a chuck to hold a

When sawing a circle with an edge guide used as a trammel beam, wedge the kerf as you near end of cut

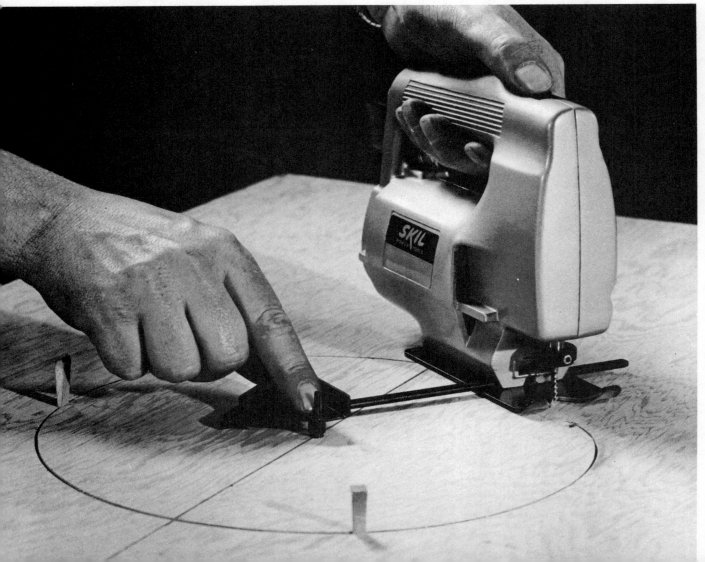

blade on its lower end. But in size, power, quality and price, the models differ widely. You can buy a sabre saw for under $10, or you can pay more than $100.

When considering which saw to buy, the real question is whether a more expensive tool's extra quality and features will prove, to *you,* worth the higher cost. The answer depends upon the work you'll do with the saw. In general, a better tool is a better buy, and for any given make, the model second from the top of the line is likely to be the best value.

● **Big or little?** Most light-duty saws with ⅝-in.-long strokes have motors that draw about 2.5 amps. and develop up to ¼ hp. Such saws readily cut 1-in. hardwood or 1½-in. softwood.

Heavier duty saws with 1-in.-long strokes have motors drawing up to about 4 amps. and developing around ½ hp. These larger tools can

Sears' 12-speed saw has a knob for steering the blade in any direction without need to turn the saw

To saw sheet metal smoothly, use a 32-tooth, wave-set, metal-cutting blade with a slow, even feed

When power-hacking pipe or angle iron, use the saw's slowest speed and flood the cut with light oil

For a plunge cut, rock the saw forward, then gradually pivot the tool backward until blade cuts through

Shoes on some saws slide back to permit cutting to a wall when sawing openings for ductwork

For perfectly square cuts when sawing lumber to length, use a small try square to guide the saw's shoe

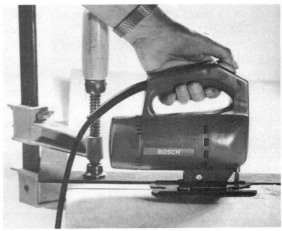

To cut panel stock with bench-saw accuracy, run the saw's shoe along a square clamped to the work

On aluminum, use a blade with teeth fine enough not to snag, but coarse enough to avoid any loading

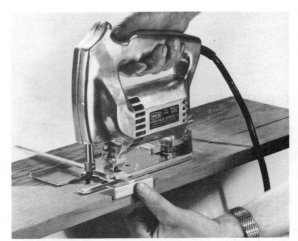

Edge guide attachment keeps saw parallel with the stock's edge and simplifies ripping of narrow strips

Notched joints can be fitted in minutes with a sabre saw. The tool is indispensible for boatbuilding

With a 6-in. blade, a 1-in.-stroke saw can notch 4 x 4s, lop tree branches, and saw openings in partitions

To cut compound-angle miters with a tilt-base saw, tilt the base and tack a wood fence to the work

Shoe insert, an attachment available for some sabre saws, reduces splintering when you cut plywood

rip 2-in. planks twice as fast as smaller models, and with extra-length blades they can cut off or notch 4x4s.

A lightweight, light-duty sabre saw is perhaps easier to handle, and if you'll use it only for light woodwork—cutting off 2x4s and sawing plywood—it's just the tool for the work.

But if you'll use your saw in construction work, a larger, faster-cutting model will be worth the extra money. A heavy-duty saw is also preferable if you'll be sawing metal. Larger models have enough power to gradually hacksaw through mild-steel plate, and because the longer stroke utilizes more of the blade's teeth, metal-cutting blades give longer service.

● **Single or multiple-speed?** A single-speed saw operating at a no-load speed of around 3000 strokes per minute is fine for light woodwork—but not much else.

Two and three-speed models, while more expensive, are more versatile. A three-speed tool generally has a medium speed of about 2500 strokes per minute and a low speed of around 2250 strokes.

Three kinds of blades will handle most work. Fast-cutting blade with alternate-set teeth (left) saws a wide kerf. A smoother cutting, taper-ground blade (center) cuts more slowly and leaves a narrower kerf. The metal-cutting blade (right) is wave-set to minimize snagging and to produce a smooth cut

sabre saws, continued

Several higher priced heavy-duty saws now have trigger-controlled continuously-variable speeds of from 0 to 3000 strokes per minute. Others have dial-type controls giving full-power speed ranges around 1300 to 3000 strokes per minute.

Slow speed is a considerable advantage. A saw chugging along smoothly at moderate speed is more pleasant to use and easier to guide than one chattering lickety-split. And slow speed makes the tool more suitable for metalwork. Even the slowest speed of some multispeed sabre saws is really too fast for heavy-duty hacksawing because even top-quality, metal-cutting blades dull rapidly when used at more than 1500 strokes per minute. Slow speed is also useful for power-filing.

● **Saw-bar action.** In most portable sabre saws the blade travels straight up and down. A mechanism in some models rocks the blade slightly as it reciprocates, giving an orbital cutting action. Orbiting, the blade bites into the work on the upstroke and clears on the downstroke. This provides better chip clearance.

In an industrial-model saw designed for fastest possible cutting, orbital action is a significant advantage. For a saw used in a home shop, it's less important. Orbital saws are more complex mechanically and higher priced, and in home shop-work the added cutting speed is hardly worth the extra cost. Besides, you can have similar fast-cutting action with a straight-line saw by using a canted blade (angled or curved slightly forward).

Smooth saw-bar action, however, is important, since a well-counterbalanced saw is much more comfortable to use than one that vibrates excessively. To check the balance of a saw you're considering, switch the tool on and feel the action.

● **Metal or plastic casing?** Some saws have die-cast aluminum casings; others have casings of injection-molded ABS plastic. A metal case makes a longer lasting tool. But any portable electric tool with a metal case should be gounded electrically to protect the operator in the event the tool should short, and this means a three-wire cable with a three-prong plug.

metal-cased saw preferable

If your shop area is properly wired with grounded receptacles, a metal-cased sabre saw is undoubtedly preferable. But if you'll be plugging into ungrounded outlets, a double-insulated plastic-cased saw is safer. Too, a plastic-cased tool is somewhat quieter.

Some manufacturers compromise, using a metal motor casing with a plastic handle—a combination used for many industrial saws. This makes the tool safe, yet satisfies anyone who still feels prejudice against plastic tools.

● **Tilt or no tilt?** Several sabre-saw models, light or heavy-duty, are available with a tilting or fixed base shoe. While a tilting shoe can be a convenience, it's a feature you'll seldom use. Sabre-sawing bevels isn't especially common.

Depending on saw design, a fixed shoe may be preferable. A nontilting shoe is more solid and lowers the saw's profile. A low-handled sabre saw is easier to guide than a high-handled one.

● **Selecting blades.** Since the blades do the cutting, it pays to buy quality ones. An inexpensive saw with a fine blade will give better performance than a more expensive saw with a cheap blade.

Many specialty blades are available for portable sabre saws, but three kinds handle most work: alternate-set blades, taper-ground blades and wave-set metal-cutting blades.

alternate-set blades for rough cuts

Alternate-set blades, with teeth swaged alternately right and left, are general-purpose blades used for rough cutting. Blades with six teeth per inch are suitable for stock more than 1 in. thick; blades with 10 teeth per inch are preferable for wood less than 1 in. thick. Alloy-steel blades stay sharp longer than carbon steel blades.

Taper-ground blades are something like hollow-ground circular saw blades. Their back edges are ground thinner than their front edges. They cut narrower kerfs than set blades and are more difficult to turn. They do make beautiful finish cuts in hardwood.

Wave-set, metal-cutting blades, though thicker, are much like hand hacksaw blades. Liberal use of cutting oil when hacksawing steel prolongs their life.

While most sabre saws use blades with standard-pattern shanks, Rockwell, Bosch and a few other makes have improved-design chucks using special blades. They grip the blade more securely, but limit your choice of blades to those supplied by the manufacturer.

In all, it's well worth shopping around before you buy a sabre saw. Look at industrial-model tools sold through industrial supply firms as well as home-shop saws sold through hardware stores. Get the best model you can afford, for your sabre saw will be one shop tool you'll use a great deal.

Let your drill press double as a lathe

BY V. P. KISNER

Your drill press can serve
as a vertical lathe. Just add
a couple of centers and a
toolrest as described here

■ IF YOU OWN a drill press, you also own a
lathe because a drill press, for all practical purposes, is a lathe that stands on end.

When you think about it, a drill press has all
the features of a lathe. Like a lathe, it has a
motor-driven spindle with a chuck that will grip
a drive center. It has a sliding worktable to which
a tailstock center can be attached and adjusted to
suit the workpiece. And it has a solid support

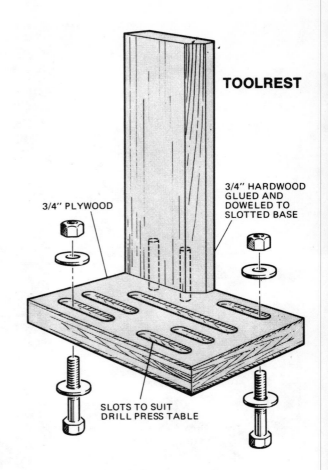

TOOLREST

3/4" HARDWOOD GLUED AND DOWELED TO SLOTTED BASE

3/4" PLYWOOD

SLOTS TO SUIT DRILL PRESS TABLE

lathe from a drill press, continued

which can be used for attaching an improvised toolrest. Presto—a lathe!

Where an occasional turning job does not warrant the investment in a lathe, your drill press will serve as a fine substitute. My bench-model drill press will handle a turning up to 17 in. long. Of course, a larger drill press will allow you to turn longer stock.

make your own centers

Headstock and tailstock centers used in a conventional wood lathe can't be used in a drill press, so you'll have to make your own centers and a toolrest. A ½-in. square-head machine bolt 5 or 6 in. long, with two hex nuts and two large washers, will make both the headstock drive center and the tailstock dead center.

The drive center is made from the head of the bolt. First saw off the bolt at a point 1½ in. from the head. Then scribe a line diagonally across the bolthead from opposite corners and center-punch and drill a ⅛-in. hole about 1 in. deep in the top of the bolt. Now make hacksaw cuts from corner-to-corner about ³⁄₁₆ in. deep and across the ⅛-in. hole. In use, the spurs of the headstock center engage kerfs in the turning to hold the work securely.

Next make a pointed stud from ⅛-in. drill rod, or a nail, which will slip freely in the center hole and project about ½ in. Make four "spurs," or lugs, preferably from hardened steel, to slip into the slots and solder them in place. (See drawing, page 110).

use hacksaw blade for fins

I made my spurs from a piece of spring salvaged from the rewind starter of a junked lawn mower. Pieces from a discarded hacksaw blade would do as well. The spurs should be cut so that they project about ³⁄₁₆ in. above the bolt-

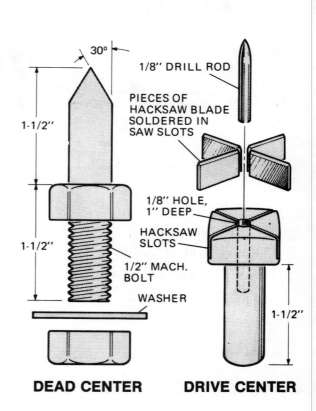

30°

1-1/2"

1-1/2"

1/2" MACH. BOLT

WASHER

DEAD CENTER

1/8" DRILL ROD

PIECES OF HACKSAW BLADE SOLDERED IN SAW SLOTS

1/8" HOLE, 1" DEEP

HACKSAW SLOTS

1-1/2"

DRIVE CENTER

Dead center, which fits a hole in the drill-press table, is rough-ground on a grinding wheel

The pointed end is then finish-ground by chucking the bolt in a drill-press and filing to a perfect point

head for proper grip on the work being turned.

To solder the parts, work some paste flux down into the center hole and the slots. You can hold the spurs in place, tight against the center stud, by wrapping thin wire around them. Grip the shank with a pair of cam-action, clamp-type pliers and apply heat below the bolthead with a propane torch. Touch a length of wire solder to the top of the assembly; when the solder melts, it will be drawn down into the hole and the slots.

To make the dead center, hacksaw off the threaded end of the bolt about 1½ in. above the threads. Grind the section above the threads to a 30–60° point. This is done by first rough-grinding it on a bench grinder with the bolt held in a ½-in. keyless chuck screwed onto the end of a work arbor to serve as a handle. You can also point it by chucking the bolt in the drill press, running the machine and grinding the end with a small stone chucked in an electric drill. After rough-grinding, the stud is chucked in the drill press and the point finished true and smooth with a fine file. Finally, the point is polished with fine emery and crocus cloth.

align dead center and drive center

The hex nuts and washers are used to clamp the pointed stud in the center hole of the table. Be sure the dead center is located precisely under the drive center. A 60° rosehead countersink can be used for recessing the workpiece so it will seat on the dead center.

The other item you'll have to make is the toolrest. This consists of a solid base with open slots so it can be bolted to the drill-press table. Make it from ¾-in. plywood or hardwood and attach the upright piece to the base with a couple of dowels and epoxy cement. The size and arrangement of the slots for bolting the rest to the table must suit your drill press. You probably will want to make two toolrests—one about 7 or 8 in. tall, which will take care of most jobs you'll encounter, and the other tall enough to take care of the longest work your drill press will accommodate.

setting up the job

You set up a turning job on the drill press the same as you would for a conventional wood lathe, by marking the center of each end of the workpiece and preparing the ends for the drive and dead centers. Tap the drive center into the workpiece, and apply a squirt of oil to the recess into which the dead center will rest. Insert the shank of the drive center in the chuck and tighten securely. Bring the spindle down until the lower end of the workpiece is seated on the dead center and lock the spindle. As the turning wears on the dead center, it may be necessary to compensate for it by lowering the spindle occasionally. There should be no play of the work between centers.

Adjust the toolrest as close to the workpiece as possible and position it so the turning chisel will be at the center line of the work. Run the press at a fairly slow speed for roughing, then shift to a higher speed for finishing. Wear goggles for safety, and keep your turning chisels honed to a razor's edge.

Fold-up toter
for hobby projects

BY SHELDON M. GALLAGER

■ IF YOU ENJOY kit-building and model-making but don't have a permanent place for such activities, here's a portable work center you can set up and put away quickly as needed. The tool-and-parts caddy can be placed on a desk, dining table or other surface for temporary use, then folded up for easy storage in a closet. Small parts are kept neatly sorted in lift-out muffin tins that can be switched to suit whatever project you're working on. One tin might hold parts for a hi-fi kit, another those for a model plane or car.

The toter consists of two hinged panels that open out to form a sturdy A-frame stand. The panels are made of perforated hardboard (Pegboard) screwed to ¾-inch-square framing strips. Using standard Pegboard fixtures, you can arrange the panels to hold any assortment of tools you like. Put the most frequently used items on the front where they're readily accessible. The back panel can store special tools and extra supplies.

You can, of course, make the carrier any size you wish. The dimensions shown here are based on a six-compartment muffin tin that typically measures about 7 by 10 inches. The tin is held in a plywood shelf that protrudes through an opening in the front panel and is hinged to a cleat screwed to the back panel. To collapse the carrier, you simply remove the parts tray, swing the shelf up between the two panels, then fold the panels flat together. Rubber stick-on feet keep the panels from slipping when opened, and screen-door hooks hold them together when closed.

Note that the cleat supporting the rear edge of the hinged shelf is 1 inch wide, projecting slightly beyond the ¾-inch thickness of the back-panel framing. This provides necessary clearance for the shelf to swing up between the panels without striking the fixture hooks that stick through on the inside of the back panel. It also allows space for two or three empty muffin tins to be left stacked in the shelf in the closed position.

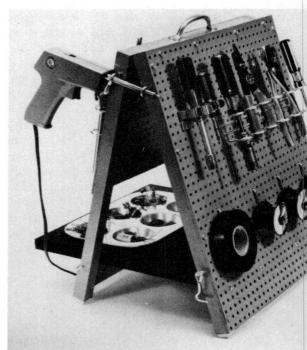

Simple holder for a hot soldering gun or pencil iron can be made from two screw eyes, one in each panel edge. Locate the eyes so they hold tool at slight downward-tipped angle to keep it from sliding out

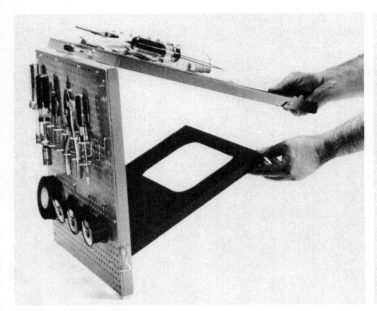
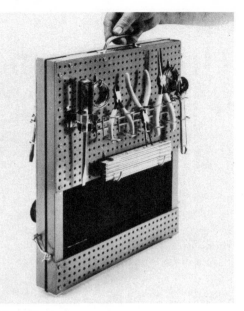

Collapsing the caddy for storage is simple. You just slip parts shelf out of opening in front panel (left, above) and swing it upward between framing strips in rear panel. Two panels then fold flat together and hook (right). A rule held in U-shaped hooks across front is handy for measuring wire lengths in electronic kit-building; you can hold the wire up to it without even removing the rule from the side of the board

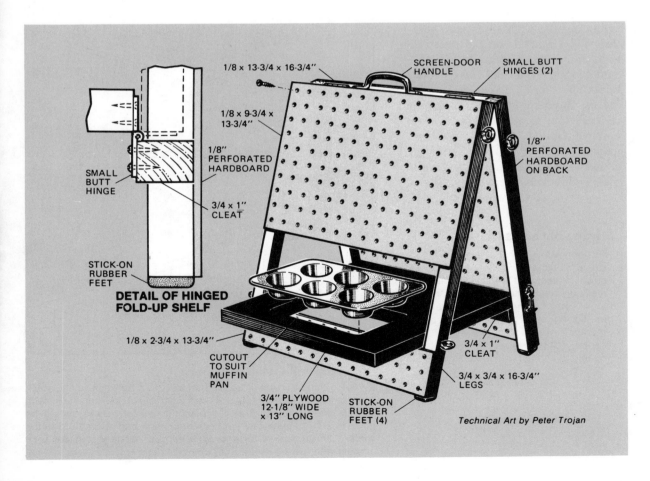

1/8 x 13-3/4 x 16-3/4"

SCREEN-DOOR HANDLE

SMALL BUTT HINGES (2)

1/8 x 9-3/4 x 13-3/4"

1/8" PERFORATED HARDBOARD

SMALL BUTT HINGE

3/4 x 1" CLEAT

1/8" PERFORATED HARDBOARD ON BACK

STICK-ON RUBBER FEET

DETAIL OF HINGED FOLD-UP SHELF

1/8 x 2-3/4 x 13-3/4"

CUTOUT TO SUIT MUFFIN PAN

3/4 x 1" CLEAT

3/4 x 3/4 x 16-3/4" LEGS

3/4" PLYWOOD 12-1/8" WIDE x 13" LONG

STICK-ON RUBBER FEET (4)

Technical Art by Peter Trojan

How to frame a basement partition

■ WHETHER YOU DECIDE to use your basement as a family funroom or leave the foundation walls bare and lay out the space to provide areas for specific family interests—workshop, sewing center or the like —it's a pretty safe bet that you'll get more efficient use from that room by installing walls. The basics of such carpentry are shown on these pages. The important point to keep in mind —if this is your first crack at doing it yourself—is to be sure to spend the time that you should in planning and laying out the walls. A typical partition wall (right) is of 2x4 construction, but since these walls are non-load-bearing, you can save a few bucks by using 2x3s. The door opening is standard; you may need a shorter door if the ceiling in your basement is low. If, like most basements your floor is uneven, you can compensate by shimming the bottom plate with wood undercourse shingles.

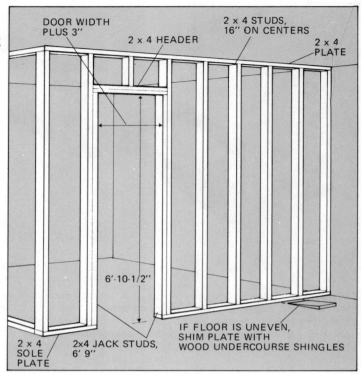

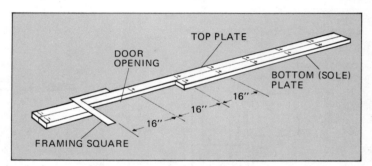

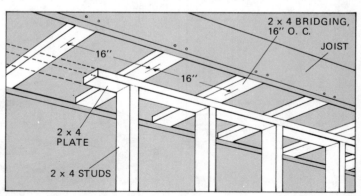

Laying out studs

Partition walls can be erected by using single plates at bottom and top. Use long stock (at least 10-footers) for this chore, making certain that it's free of twist and bow. After cutting the plates to the required length, lay them side by side and mark off the stud locations (16 in. on center). Cut away portions for the door openings on the bottom plates only

Providing solid nailing

If your partition wall will be parallel with and between joists, you'll have to install nailers (often called cats) between—and flush with bottom of—the joists. The minimum number of nailers should be three in a 10-ft. plate-run—put one near each end and a third at the center. Cut the nailers for a force-fit between joists and install each of them with two 10-penny (10d) common nails

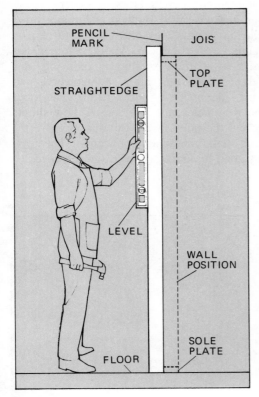

Locating top plate

To set the wall, snap a chalkline on the floor to mark the partition location. Then fasten the bottom plate in position, using either fluted masonry nails (wear safety goggles), lead anchors or masonry pins. To locate the top plate directly over the sole plate, use a straightedge (length of 2x3) and level as shown above. Plumb the straightedge and make several marks on the joists for the top plate at several points along the plate run

Building the wall

If your concrete floor is in good shape—that is, relatively level—you can assemble the studs to the top plate on the floor, then tilt the wall up into position as a unit. Check studs with your level (both vertical planes must be plumb) and fasten the top plate to joists with 10d nails spaced 16 in. o.c. But if your floor is not level, fasten the top plate only to those points marked on the joists and cut and install the studs one at a time. Stand on the sole plate to mark a stud for length, then cut the stud full (i.e., leave the line). Such a force-fit bears against the plates for rigidity; when you remove your weight, the plate springs up. You may find an assistant helpful for this part of the work

Nailing a stud

To toenail a stud, place the stud on the line on the bottom plate and about an inch or so above the plate, then drive two 8d nails at about a 60° angle. Even though you buck the board (brace it with your shoe) it will move slightly off the line; bring it back to the line by driving a third 8d nail on the opposite side. Finally, to fix the stud, drive in a fourth nail on the face, or narrow, side. Repeat the toenailing at the top if installing the studs individually as mentioned under the heading *Building the wall* in the column at the right

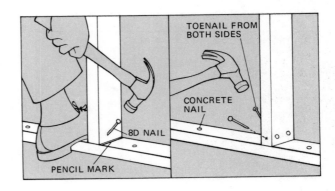

How to add an outlet

ROOMS IN OLDER HOMES never seem to have enough electrical outlets, and many times you end up using a long extension cord to plug in a lamp across the room. Adding another outlet and tying it to an existing one is a job, surprisingly enough, that many homeowners and handymen do not know how to do. The steps illustrated and described here show how simple it is to cut the hole, install the box, prepare the wire and make the actual connection. Then you can say good-by to hazardous extension cords.

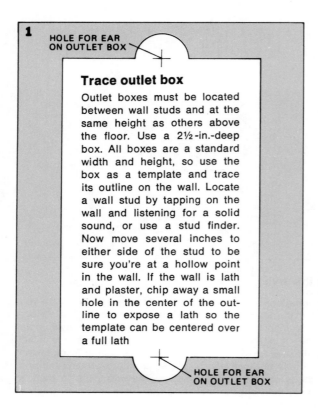

1

HOLE FOR EAR ON OUTLET BOX

Trace outlet box

Outlet boxes must be located between wall studs and at the same height as others above the floor. Use a 2½-in.-deep box. All boxes are a standard width and height, so use the box as a template and trace its outline on the wall. Locate a wall stud by tapping on the wall and listening for a solid sound, or use a stud finder. Now move several inches to either side of the stud to be sure you're at a hollow point in the wall. If the wall is lath and plaster, chip away a small hole in the center of the outline to expose a lath so the template can be centered over a full lath

HOLE FOR EAR ON OUTLET BOX

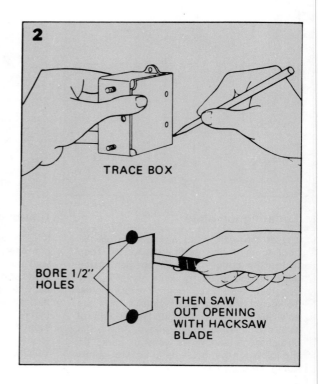

2

TRACE BOX

BORE 1/2" HOLES

THEN SAW OUT OPENING WITH HACKSAW BLADE

Anchoring outlet box in a wall

If the wall is lath and plaster, you simply attach the wood lath with small screws. If the wall is plasterboard, the box is anchored in the hole with special metal supports, as shown below. To install the metal supports, you work one along each side of the box and move it up and down against the inside surface of the wall. Then bend the projecting ears inside the box, as shown in the lower left-hand drawing. All hardware is available at electrical supply stores

Cutting hole for box

If wall is plasterboard, it's not necessary to chip hole to locate and center the box over a full lath. Simply trace around the box and drill two ½-in. holes through the wall at the top and bottom half-round notches. Similar holes are made in a lath-and-plaster wall. The box opening is cut out with a hand-held hacksaw blade. If sawing lath, draw the saw teeth toward you. Wrap the saw blade with several turns of tape for a more comfortable grip, or wear a glove. The drilled holes provide clearance for the projecting tabs at the top and bottom of all outlet boxes. They also make it easy to insert hacksaw blade or keyhole saw

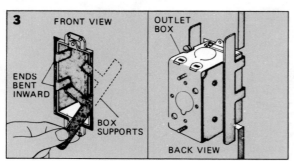

3 FRONT VIEW

OUTLET BOX

ENDS BENT INWARD

BOX SUPPORTS

BACK VIEW

How to install armored cable

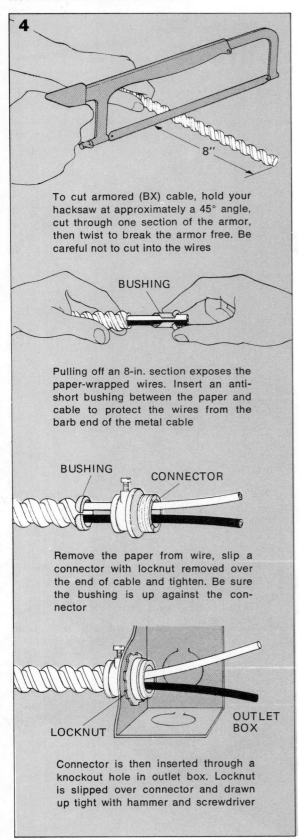

4

8″

To cut armored (BX) cable, hold your hacksaw at approximately a 45° angle, cut through one section of the armor, then twist to break the armor free. Be careful not to cut into the wires

BUSHING

Pulling off an 8-in. section exposes the paper-wrapped wires. Insert an anti-short bushing between the paper and cable to protect the wires from the barb end of the metal cable

BUSHING   CONNECTOR

Remove the paper from wire, slip a connector with locknut removed over the end of cable and tighten. Be sure the bushing is up against the connector

LOCKNUT   OUTLET BOX

Connector is then inserted through a knockout hole in outlet box. Locknut is slipped over connector and drawn up tight with hammer and screwdriver

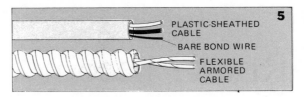

5

PLASTIC-SHEATHED CABLE

BARE BOND WIRE

FLEXIBLE ARMORED CABLE

Two kinds of cable you can use

You have a choice of using armored cable or plastic cable to wire your new outlet. Armored (also called BX) has a flexible-steel covering that requires a hacksaw to cut. The covering on plastic cable can be cut with a knife and it's easy to pull and strip. The national code requires a cable having a bond wire, as shown above. In the case of armored cable, the cable armor itself serves as the bond. In the case of plastic-sheathed cable, a separate bonding wire is attached to the outlet box with a screw or special clip, or the cable is connected to a box that's equipped with a bonding jumper. Thus your new outlet will have continuous bond, provided the rest of the system was originally bonded. Be sure that when you connect the cable to the terminals on the old outlet that you connect black wire to black wire and white wire to white

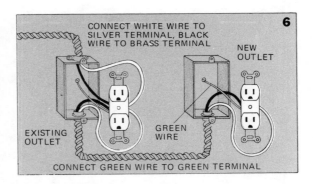

6

CONNECT WHITE WIRE TO SILVER TERMINAL, BLACK WIRE TO BRASS TERMINAL

NEW OUTLET

EXISTING OUTLET

GREEN WIRE

CONNECT GREEN WIRE TO GREEN TERMINAL

Routing the cable from box to box

How you run the cable from existing box to new one depends on where the boxes are located. If they're on the same wall, you can remove the baseboard, notch each stud to accept the cable and cover with metal kick plates for protection. If boxes are on different walls and there's a basement below, it's easier to bore up into the walls from underneath and run the cable across under the joists. If the new outlet is on the other side of a doorway, the cable can be concealed behind the trim, usually by chipping out the plaster or wallboard, and run up and over the door. Be careful, though, in reattaching the trim not to nail into the cable. To connect the cable to the old box, pry open a knockout and fish a thin wire through the hole to pull the cable into the box. Most important of all is to always remember to turn off the electricity before making the final connections

Router becomes a shaper

Build this cabinet for your router and
you'll have an instant shaper for your shop.   Here's how to do it

BY WALTER E. BURTON

IF YOU TURN a portable router upside down, you have, essentially, a wood-working shaper. To do it, the inverted router must be supported in such a way that it can function as a shaper with work guides, guards and the like. This shop-built version was designed to accommodate a Millers Falls MF router, Model A, catalog No. 7200. But, where necessary, dimensions can be altered for your own router.

The router hangs suspended from the underside of the cabinet top so that it can be removed for conventional routing operations by unscrewing four nuts. The hinged top tilts upward for convenience in changing cutters and making adjustments—although you can make cutter-height settings by reaching into the cabinet.

The cabinet top is hinged to the rear panel. Centered on the top is a $\frac{1}{16}$ x 8 x 8-in. aluminum plate that rests in a recess so the plate surface and adjacent wood are in the same plane. The hole at plate center is approximately 1⅛ in. in diameter. In the wood top, concentric with this

The router cuts a recess in the cabinet top to hold the plate against which router base is clamped

Bottom of the top panel: The router is clamped against the metal plate

In the partially assembled cabinet, the accessory drawer and some vent openings for airflow are seen

For installing or removing the router, the cabinet is flipped on its back and top panel swung open

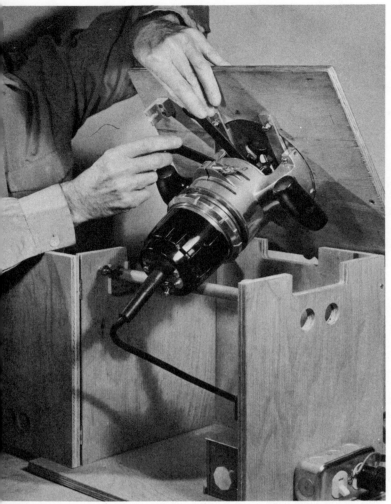

To change cutters, the router is swung up and held by
a dowel engaging sockets on the side panels

router becomes a shaper, continued

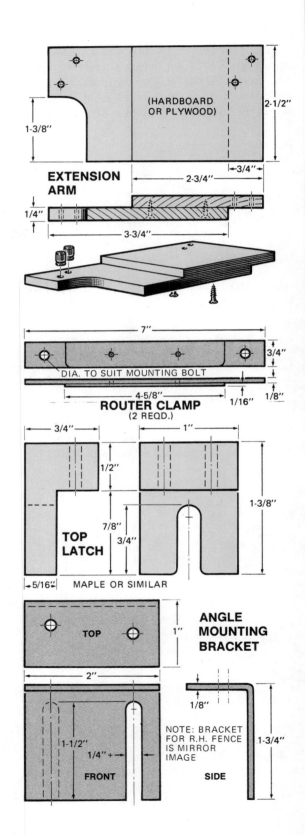

EXTENSION
ARM

(HARDBOARD
OR PLYWOOD)

2-1/2"
1-3/8"
3/4"
2-3/4"
1/4"
3-3/4"

ROUTER CLAMP
(2 REQD.)

7"
3/4"
DIA. TO SUIT MOUNTING BOLT
4-5/8"
1/16"
1/8"

TOP
LATCH

3/4"
1/2"
1"
1-3/8"
7/8"
3/4"
5/16"
MAPLE OR SIMILAR

ANGLE
MOUNTING
BRACKET

TOP
1"
2"
1-1/2"
1/4" +
FRONT

1/8"
NOTE: BRACKET
FOR R.H. FENCE
IS MIRROR
IMAGE
1-3/4"
SIDE

hole, is a 6-in.-dia. opening for the router base.
Check your router's shoe diameter before cutting
this circle.

You can form the $\frac{1}{16}$-in.-deep recess by routing out most of the area with a straight bit. Leave
an "island" in the center until last so the router
shoe is supported. Then, remove the island with
a router bit in a drill press. Next, jigsaw the 6-in.
opening. Fasten the plate in its recess with two
countersunk wood screws near the opposite
corners.

To determine the center of the 1⅛-in. hole,
insert a pointed cutter in the router and place
the router base into its opening. The point where

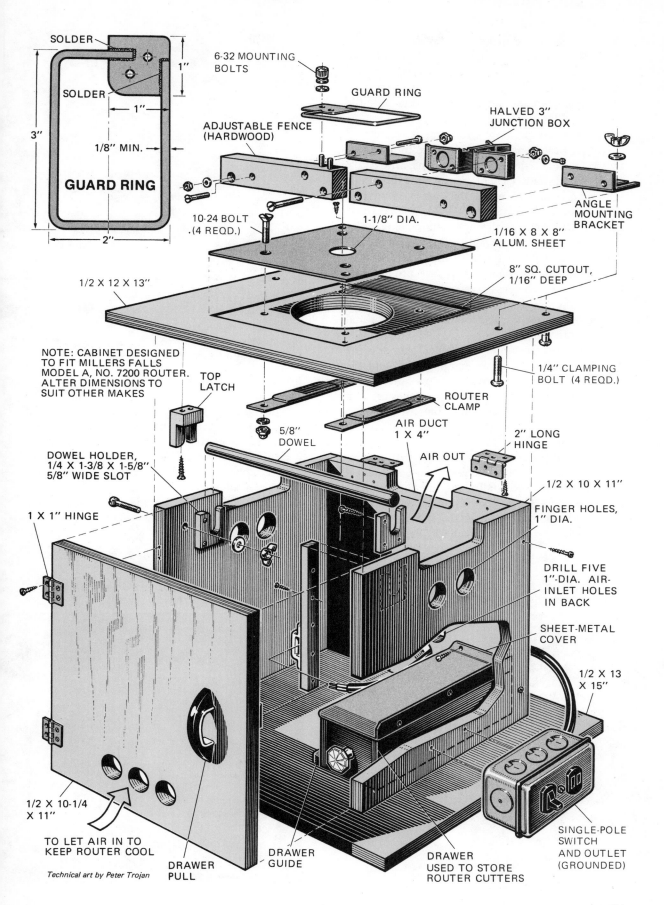

SOLDER

1"

SOLDER

6-32 MOUNTING BOLTS

GUARD RING

3"

1"

1/8" MIN.

GUARD RING

2"

ADJUSTABLE FENCE (HARDWOOD)

HALVED 3" JUNCTION BOX

ANGLE MOUNTING BRACKET

10-24 BOLT .(4 REQD.)

1-1/8" DIA.

1/16 X 8 X 8" ALUM. SHEET

1/2 X 12 X 13"

8" SQ. CUTOUT, 1/16" DEEP

NOTE: CABINET DESIGNED TO FIT MILLERS FALLS MODEL A, NO. 7200 ROUTER. ALTER DIMENSIONS TO SUIT OTHER MAKES

TOP LATCH

1/4" CLAMPING BOLT (4 REQD.)

ROUTER CLAMP

AIR DUCT 1 X 4"

5/8" DOWEL

2" LONG HINGE

AIR OUT

1/2 X 10 X 11"

DOWEL HOLDER, 1/4 X 1-3/8 X 1-5/8" 5/8" WIDE SLOT

FINGER HOLES, 1" DIA.

1 X 1" HINGE

DRILL FIVE 1"-DIA. AIR-INLET HOLES IN BACK

SHEET-METAL COVER

1/2 X 13 X 15"

1/2 X 10-1/4 X 11"

TO LET AIR IN TO KEEP ROUTER COOL

SINGLE-POLE SWITCH AND OUTLET (GROUNDED)

Technical art by Peter Trojan

DRAWER PULL

DRAWER GUIDE

DRAWER USED TO STORE ROUTER CUTTERS

121

the bit touches the metal plate is the center for the hole. Use two 2-in. butt hinges to join top to back panel. Although the router's weight will hold the top down, rigidity is increased by installing a simple wooden latch at the corner near the front panel hinge.

The router-mounting arrangement is dictated by router-base construction. For the tool shown, two ⅛ x ¾ x 7-in. aluminum strips, with 1/16 x ¾ x 4⅝-in. pads (to compensate for difference in router base and wood thickness) riveted to them, worked fine. Four 10–24 bolts extend through these strips, through countersunk holes in the metal top insert and plywood and are secured to the cabinet top with nuts and washers.

The cabinet and cabinet-top sizes are not critical. The dimensions given provide adequate space, although the power cord must be curved sideways in order to clear the bottom at the usual cutter depth settings.

Since a router motor "breathes" by drawing air in at cord-end and discharging it around the cutter, it's a must to provide airflow holes in the box. These consist of 1x4-in. notches at top edges of the sidepieces and back panel and multiple 1-in. holes in the back and front panels. (The two 1-in. holes at the top of each side are primarily finger holes for carrying.) If the intake air seems to carry excessive dust and chips, it's a good idea to install some fine-mesh screen over the inlets. Chips should not be permitted to build up in the box; if the router is to be used for long periods, periodically check the motor to

Interior view shows the router in operating position. Plastic shield was replaced by the ring type

avoid overheating. If necessary, leave the door open.

The hinged top can be raised to give better access to the router when you change cutters. The router is held in the tilted position by resting it on a piece of ⅝-in. dowel whose ends engage notched plywood pieces screwed to the inside surfaces of sidepieces.

The storage drawer is made of ¼-in. plywood and is located in one corner of the cabinet. To keep it in position, glue a guide strip along the

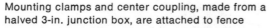
Mounting clamps and center coupling, made from a halved 3-in. junction box, are attached to fence

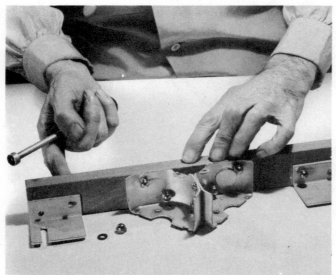

Rear of guide fence is in position for straightedged work. Notice ring-type shield in foreground

bottom. A sheet-aluminum cover helps keep dirt out and the drawer in place. Inside, a wooden block drilled to receive cutter shanks holds stored cutters.

An adjustable fence guides straightedged work past the cutter. I used a piece of maple cut to the dimensions indicated. An angle mounting bracket was then fastened to each end with bolts.

An adjustable bracket assembly made from a 3-in. electrical junction box (sawed diagonally in two) is bolted to the fence center. A little hammering and filing will let you fit the box halves squarely with the surfaces at a right angle and parallel where they contact the wood. Three 8–32 bolts hold the two halves together; holes in one of them are slotted so the guide fence can be adjusted for cut depth when jointing.

After bolting the junction-box bracket assembly to the wooden strip, saw a section slightly over 1 in. wide from the center of the strip to provide space for the cutter. Normally, the fence is used with surfaces of both halves in the same plane, but they can be offset as desired—by loosening the bolts holding the junction-box halves together. The fence assembly is centered with respect to the cutter, and holes for the ¼-in. clamping bolts are located near edges of the cabinet top. A second set of holes is drilled near the back edge of the top to provide an alternate fence position.

Make a guard ring to fit over the fence gap, which can also be used on an extension arm when nonstraight edges are being shaped. The loop,

made from ⅛-in. rod, is soldered to a brass plate drilled for 6–32 mounting bolts. The extension arm, made from ¼-in. plywood, is stepped to bring it nearer the cutter and improve rigidity. Bolts holding the guard and extension arm should be in one half of the guide fence only so you can adjust the other half for depth of cut.

Because the router switch is not easily reached when the cabinet door is closed, you'll need an outside control. This consists of a single-pole switch and outlet (provided with ground connection) housed in a surface-mounting switch box screwed to the cabinet side. The router is plugged into the outlet.

A sizable assortment of cutters suitable for forming edge moldings, smoothing edges and other shaping chores is available. For use without a guide fence, as in cutting moldings along irregular edges, there are bits with pilots or shoulders to limit the cut. The setup illustrated had no tendency to "walk" because vibration is light. If desired, you can use C-clamps to anchor the cabinet on a table or bench.

Fingers should, of course, be kept away from cutters. Instead, various work hold-downs—such as springy steel strips—can be designed as needed, mounted on the fence and supplemented by push sticks to hold work against the cutter.

Your shaper cabinet can be finished conventionally. For the top, an easy finish is a sealer, such as thinned shellac, followed by two polish coats of floor wax. The rest of the cabinet can be varnished or painted.

To shape edges on straight work, a ring-type shield is mounted on the rear fence to protect fingers

For curved work, guide fence is moved to the back position. Ring guard is mounted on the extension

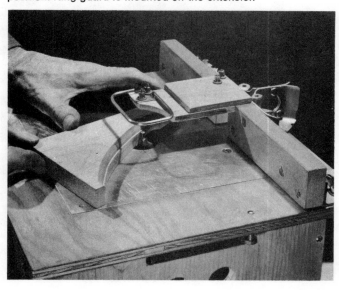

Build a beautiful octagon lamp table

BY WAYNE C. LECKEY

Inexpensive 'hand-carved' panels glued to its sides
give this octagon lamp table a handsome $100 look

■ NOTHING GIVES home-built furniture the look of elegance more quickly than molded reproductions of hand-carved panels. A good example is this handsome lamp table. Team up the panels with decorative laminate and a portable router, and this project will stack up with the best at any furniture store.

The table begins as a plain plywood shell. But when exposed plywood surfaces are covered with wood-grain decorative laminate and molded panels are added to all eight sides, your piece will look anything but homemade.

To start the octagon base, cut eight 10x20¼-in. panels from ¾-in. fir plywood, but don't bevel the edges. Next cut and cement pieces of decorative wood-grain laminate to the panels—top, bottom and center. The center piece can be scrap. Use contact cement to stick the laminate

flush with the edges and run the grain crosswise.

Tilt your table saw to cut a 22½° (or 67½°) angle and slowly bevel the two side edges on each panel. Use a carbide-tip blade so you won't chip the laminate. Finished width of each panel should be 9$\frac{13}{16}$ in.—actual width of molded panel.

Special clamp nails, hammered into saw kerfs, are used to assemble the eight into an octagon shell. To cut kerfs in the beveled edges, return the blade to 90°, set it for a ¼-in.-deep cut and run a kerf (⅛ in. wide) full length down the center of the bevel. Hold the plywood with the bevel flat on the table and the point of the bevel against the saw fence. Clamp nails draw the joint together as they are hammered in. Apply glue to joints.

Lay out the tabletop on a piece of ¾-in. fir

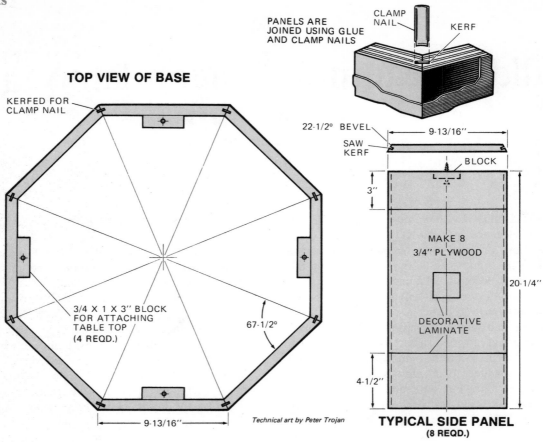

TOP VIEW OF BASE

KERFED FOR
CLAMP NAIL

PANELS ARE
JOINED USING GLUE
AND CLAMP NAILS

CLAMP
NAIL

KERF

22-1/2° BEVEL

SAW
KERF

9-13/16''

BLOCK

3''

MAKE 8
3/4'' PLYWOOD

20-1/4''

3/4 X 1 X 3'' BLOCK
FOR ATTACHING
TABLE TOP
(4 REQD.)

67-1/2°

DECORATIVE
LAMINATE

4-1/2''

9-13/16''

Technical art by Peter Trojan

TYPICAL SIDE PANEL
(8 REQD.)

plywood by striking a 12⅛-in. radius and drawing an octagon. Carefully miter an edging of solid wood (¾ x 1-in. walnut) and glue it to the plywood all around (see drawing, page 127), flush with the top. The edging hides the plywood edges and provides solid stock for shaping.

To cover the top, cut decorative laminate in octagon shape roughly 25¾ in. across. When you cement it in place, keep it centered, ¼ in. in from the edge.

To rout the ⅛-in. decorative surface groove around the top, you'll need a jig. It's simply an octagonal ring of ¾ x 1-in. pieces made to fit the perimeter of the top. All joints of the jig are glued except one—left open (³⁄₁₆ in.) so the jig can be pulled with a C-clamp to hold it in place. Here a couple of ears (wood blocks) glued to each side of the open joint will accommodate the clamp. Notice that the jig is positioned to project ¼ in. above the top to provide a lip for the router base. The groove is made with a ⅛-in. veining bit set to just barely cut into the laminate —not more than half its thickness. Distance of the groove from the edge is determined by the router's base diameter. If it's 5 in., the groove would be 2½ in. from the edge.

Shaping the outer edge completes the top. The original was shaped with a Stanley No. 5708 cut-

ter. In detail A the thickness of the laminate provides the ¹⁄₁₆-in. shoulder of the profile. Take about three passes to shape the complete profile and move the router slowly, particularly when you start cutting into the laminate. Carefully hand-sand the edge.

Carved panels are glued in place one at a time with contact cement. Apply the cement to the very edge of each panel, top and bottom, and decorative laminate (none along side edges of the molded panels). Also apply cement to the center panels and laminate scraps. The first panel must be positioned squarely if the final one is to align properly with the rest. It's wise to make a dry run by fastening all eight panels in place with tabs of masking tape. Then apply guide placement strips of masking tape to the laminate along the top and bottom edges to be assured of perfect alignment of all eight. If the plywood panels of the shell were cut and joined accurately, the carved panels should fit with no space showing between abutting edges. If you wish, the plywood can be stained dark along the joints before the panels are cemented in place.

The top is attached to the base with screws through four wood blocks glued to the base on the inside at the top.

We used Johns-Manville Melamite laminate

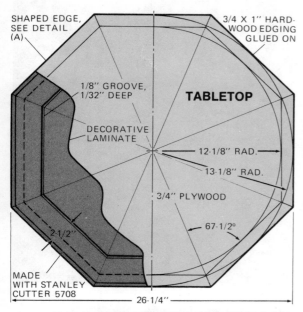

SHAPED EDGE, SEE DETAIL (A)

3/4 X 1" HARD-WOOD EDGING GLUED ON

1/8" GROOVE, 1/32" DEEP

TABLETOP

DECORATIVE LAMINATE

12-1/8" RAD.

13-1/8" RAD.

3/4" PLYWOOD

67-1/2°

2-1/2"

MADE WITH STANLEY CUTTER 5708

26-1/4"

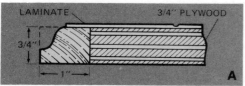

LAMINATE   3/4" PLYWOOD

3/4"

1"

A

Band of contact cement is applied to the laminate along edge of masking tape with a small paintbrush

Contact cement is also applied to back of carved panels at the center and along top and bottom edges

When the cement is dry to the touch (about 20 minutes), the carved panel is positioned

to cover the table: Carpathian burl on top, and ranch pecan on the sides. The eight carved panels can be purchased for about $22 postpaid from United Southern Associates, Box 5521, High Point, N.C. 26262. To get the right color, ask for panel KR-50070.

The only part that needs hand finishing is the shaped edge. After sanding it smooth, apply walnut stain and let dry. Then apply two coats of Pierce-Stevens Wood Lore or Gaston's waxing lacquer, sanding lightly between coats. Finally, apply stain only to the 1/8-in. groove in the top with a small brush.

Wood ring clamped to perimeter provides fence for router to make a 1/8 in. groove in laminate

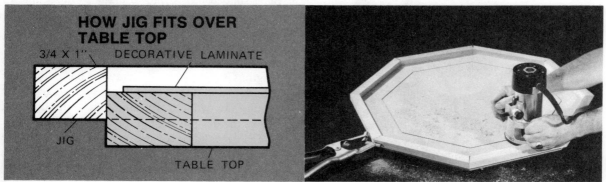

HOW JIG FITS OVER TABLE TOP

3/4 X 1"   DECORATIVE LAMINATE

JIG

TABLE TOP

craft projects

'Turning' spirals on a lathe

Of course you can't really
turn spirals on a lathe,
but here's a handy technique
using the lathe as a helpful
tool for cutting spirals by hand

BY GARTH F. GRAVES

■ IT'S A GOOD TRICK if you can do it, but you really can't turn a spiral on a wood lathe. You can do basic turning, but after that it's strictly hand work with the lathe serving as a workholder.

Still, adding a twist to your lathe projects is fun and rewarding; you can give a 17th-century touch to Mediterranean-style furniture. Candlesticks and door handles shown are good examples of what a spiral can do to add individuality to your workshop projects.

A spiral can be formed around a cylinder freehand, but a pair of spiral-turned cylinders must match, requiring symmetrical paths with distances and shapes the same as spirals wind around cylinders.

If a cylinder with one spiral revolution could be rolled on a flat plane, the spiral would become a straight line, and the portion below a right triangle.

To construct a spiral path, cut a paper template shaped like a right triangle as illustrated at the right. Length of the cylinder section is the base (side B) and height (side A) is the cylinder's circumference multiplied by number of spiral revolutions wanted within the cylinder's length. Glue or tape the template base along the cylinder length; then wrap the rest of the template around the cylinder, forming a diagonal line that marks the desired path of the spiral.

The template provides a quick way to locate a spiral on smaller projects—fewer than five turns around a small-diameter cylinder. For larger diameters or more tightly wrapped grooves, this is cumbersome, so try a grid method.

To mark a spiral on a large cylinder, divide the cylinder lengthwise into four equal sections (see page 129). Mark the spiral lead along the cylinder and draw lines around the cylinder to mark off each spiral revolution. Then divide each marked section into four equal parts and draw lines around the cylinder at these points. Where horizontal and radial lines intersect along the spiral, connect these points around and along the cylinder with a flexible straightedge and mark the spiral path.

Rotation rate and groove profile both affect design. The top drawing on page 130 shows how you change this by using the same groove pattern but expanding the lead. Add another design variation to the groove pattern, and possibilities are almost limitless. For basic patterns, see page 130.

Methods described so far are for a single spiral path—one line around and along a cylinder. Multiple spiral paths in the same area create a smoother flow that may be better for certain projects. The principle of the single-spiral path is used, but it is repeated three or more times within the same cylindrical length. The center drawing on page 130 shows a spiral pattern ob-

A triangular paper template is used to mark the path of a continuing spiral on the piece to be worked

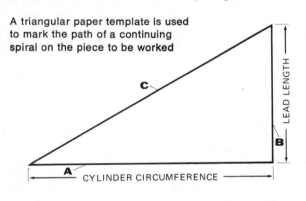

Wrap the paper template tightly around the cylinder and keep side A aligned at a base reference point to avoid distortion of the spiral path. The hypotenuse of the right triangle produces the spiral path around the cylinder to be cut

GLUE SIDE B ALONG LENGTH OF SECTION TO BE SPIRAL-TURNED

1 Divide the spiral-turned section into four equal divisions, both lengthwise and radially

2 Mark the radial divisions for the desired number of complete revolutions along the length

3 Divide the radial divisions into groups of four, then mark each group with pencil dots

4 Mark the location of intersecting axial and radial lines with a dot as you progress around the cylinder

5 Mark the spiral path using a flexible straight-edge to connect the series of intersecting dots

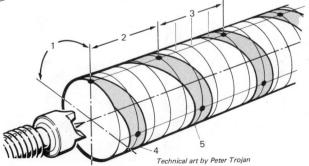

Technical art by Peter Trojan

129

This drawing shows a spiral groove traveling one complete revolution within the axial distance of:

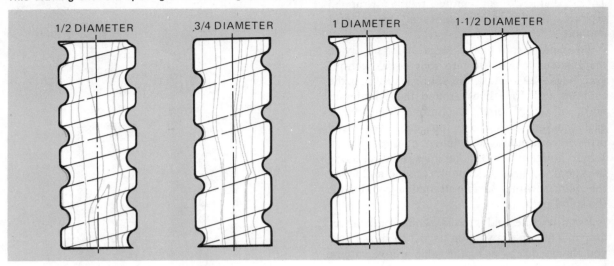

1/2 DIAMETER   3/4 DIAMETER   1 DIAMETER   1-1/2 DIAMETER

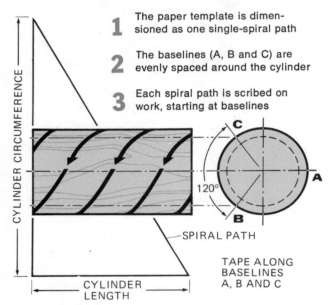

1 The paper template is dimensioned as one single-spiral path

2 The baselines (A, B and C) are evenly spaced around the cylinder

3 Each spiral path is scribed on work, starting at baselines

CYLINDER CIRCUMFERENCE

SPIRAL PATH

TAPE ALONG BASELINES A, B AND C

120°

CYLINDER LENGTH

tained when the template is used to mark three paths starting on different baselines. Determine template size, then divide the cylinder lengthwise in three equal parts (120° each). This is easily done by dividing the line representing the circumference (diameter x 3.1416) in thirds. Mark one horizontal baseline on the cylinder, tape base of the triangle template along this line, wrap template around the cylinder and mark the spiral path. Locate and mark the other two paths this way. Each will be equally spaced.

The actual spiral-cutting job is shown in the step-by-step photos on page 131. Rough-turn the cylinder but leave its diameter a bit oversize.

Spiral pattern designs are limitless. Classic patterns shown include (left to right) half-round groove, elliptical groove, continuous bead, V-groove and wide V-groove. All of them are illustrated at one revolution with the lateral distance of one diameter for comparison

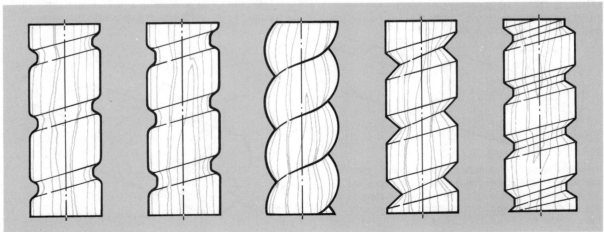

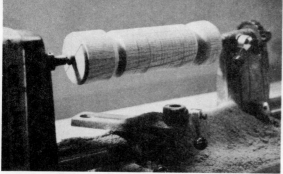

A lathe is used to turn the work to a cylindrical shape, then used only as a holding fixture. Initially, the cylinder is made oversize and turned to final size after the spiral groove is completed in the body

A spiral path is marked by drawing a continuous line which intersects longitudinal and radial grid points. If the size of the cylinder permits, you can use an alternate triangle method of marking the spiral

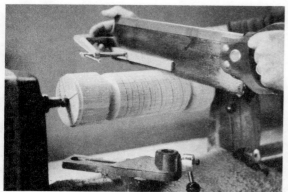

The spiral path is cut to a predetermined depth with a fine-tooth hacksaw. A wood strip clamped to blade limits depth of cut. The kerf is used as a gauge when filing the spiral groove to proper depth

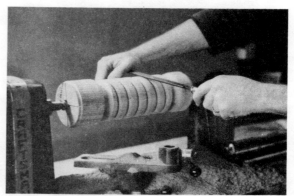

Severe chipping is prevented by breaking (chamfering) the edges of the saw kerfs with a fine file before the spiral groove is formed. If not done, a coarse rasp will chip certain woods and spoil the job

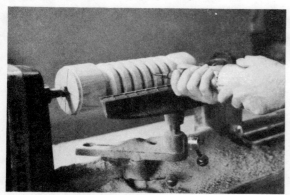

The spiral groove is cut fastest and easiest with an electric hand grinder and burr cutter. If these tools aren't available, the groove can be filed by hand. The work is turned by hand while being filed

The spiral groove is hand-sanded to a smooth finish after filing. After this the lathe is switched on, and the cylinder is turned to the final size. The cylinder is then sanded and finish applied

Turning it to final diameter after the spiral is shaped will remove chips and miscues.

When using a template, scribe the spiral path with a saw, knife or tracing wheel. To cut the spiral line to uniform depth, use a fine-tooth saw with a depth stop clamped to the blade. Saw to proper depth gradually as you go around the cylinder. The cut should rise to match the diameter of the neighboring section at each end of the spiral section.

To mark width of the spiral groove, scribe and cut additional guide lines on each side of the initial cut. To prevent deep splintering and chipping when you file the groove, first round edges of the outer cuts with a fine file. A power hand grinder will shape the groove quickly, or you can use files and rasps.

After forming the groove, turn the cylinder to its final form, sand it well and apply a suitable finish.

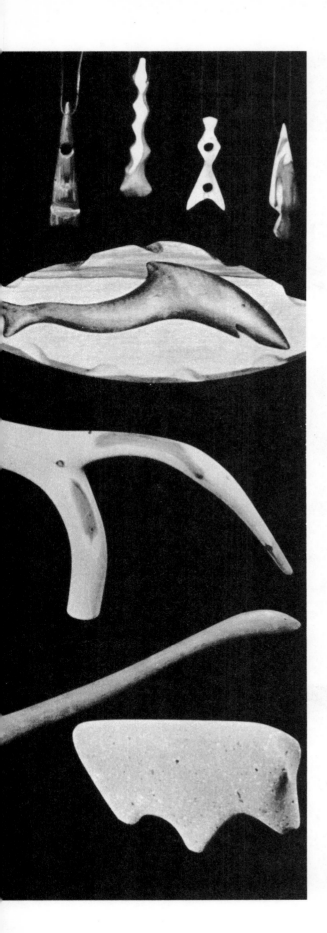

Anyone can sculpture wood

BY HARRY WICKS

■ AS YOU GUIDE the tool across the wood surface, the cutting action feels different—probably unlike that of any tool you have worked with. You quickly sense that stock removal is by shaving rather than by scraping. And on your first try with one of these tools, you feel a

wood sculpturing, continued

WRONG
WORK WILL CHATTER AND SPLINTER

RIGHT
START HERE, PULL WORK THROUGH

SURFORM DRUM

WORK-PIECE

WORK-PIECE

Necklaces are created by shaping wood pendants in abstract form, then stringing

1. Owl subject is drawn on paper, then cut out and pinned to wood. Make the outline with a felt-tip pen

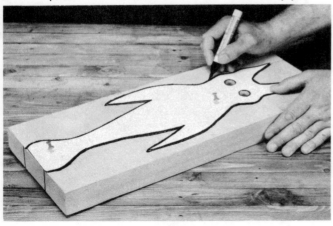

2. Fastest method of cutting block is with a bandsaw. Youngsters should use safer coping saw

3. Next step is to tack pattern to cutout. The wood being used for this carving is a softwood

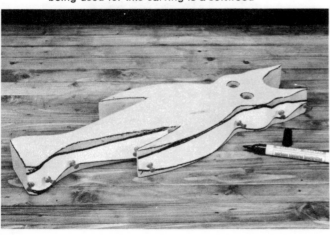

4. Concave areas are cleared using the round file. If you have a drill press, use the drum tool

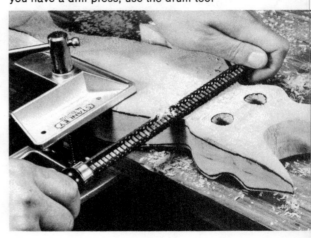

satisfying control—especially as the block of wood takes shape under your hands—that you've never felt with an ordinary plane or file. You are creating your first sculpture with Surform tools.

The pieces of sculpture shown in the color photographs are by John Matthews, British sculptor, author and crafts teacher, who developed the techniques described here. Perhaps more than any other individual, he has championed the use of Surform tools in creative arts. His latest book on the subject is *Sculpture With Surform Tools*. (For more information about

The completed owl appears on a fireplace mantel. Base is shaped from same wood, and "leg" is dowel

The drum tool chucked in a drill press makes many of the steps easier if used properly

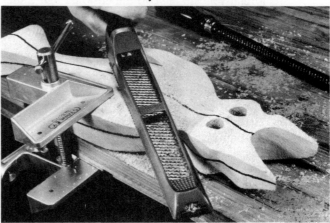

5. Midlines are drawn down center of front, back and both sides. Now contour body with a flat blade

6. Newest Surform is the only one that removes stock by pulling action. It works well on convex surfaces

7. Sandpaper wrapped around a split-dowel, or commercial sanding drum is used for final smoothing

After starting with two and three-dimensional carving, John Matthews went on to the more challenging forms found in branch sculpture. It's something like cloud gazing, he says. Just as cloud formations appear to take recognizable shapes, so do branches. Matthews "saw" the anteater in the limb he's cutting at right. The beauty of this art form is its purity; nothing is added. In fact, the trick is to know when to stop removing twigs and bark so as not to lose a good, abstract shape. There's no need to cut living branches. Those removed from fallen trees or acquired by routine pruning afford a plentiful supply

the book write Edward Arnold Ltd., 41 Maddox St., London, England.)

The best bet for your first attempt at carving is a relatively simple two-dimensional figure such as the plaque-mounted dolphin on page 133. Because you are concerned with the surface only in two-dimensional carving, you will be able to give greater attention to mastering the tools and techniques. As proficiency increases, you'll automatically graduate to more involved three-dimensional carving—animals, heads and the like. (Strictly speaking, any style of wood-carving is three-dimensional. We are using John Matthews' terms, "two-dimensional" and "three-dimensional," as a simple means of differentiating between flat-on-one-side sculpture and full-round sculpture.)

Finally, you will probably yield to the urge to try free-form branch sculpture. Then you'll be hooked for good.

Surform tools can be used on a variety of materials, including stone and some types of soft brick. Wood for a carving should be selected so as to further enhance the subject. The wild grain of fir, for example, can be utilized in over-all design, but the material is rather difficult to carve. Matthews' favorite materials are limba, African mahoganies, and other exotic woods. These are available from craftsman supply houses such as Albert Constantine & Son, 2050 Eastchester Rd., Bronx, N.Y.

There are a number of sources for subject inspiration: magazine photos, books, paintings or an encyclopedia. After selecting the subject, sketch it to actual size. Cut out this pattern and

As described in the text there is a Surform tool for every job in sculpturing. In the top photo is the Mini-file (left) which lets you get into angle where boards meet. The shaver (right) will even smooth off the end grain. Five standard Surforms are at bottom

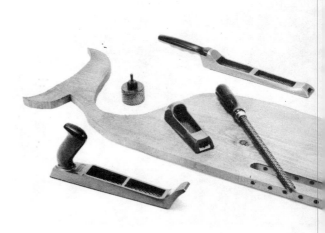

transfer it to the carving block, as shown in photos 1–3 on page 134.

The owl shown is a typical example of three-dimensional sculpture. Patterns for front and side views are drawn and cut out. The front profile is traced onto the wood, then cut out with a bandsaw, sabre saw, or—if you're teaching a youngster—a coping saw. The procedure is repeated for the side profile.

remove the excess

Removal of excess material with Surform tools is next. If possible, use the drum tool for large areas and concave surfaces. Or use the round file. (The tools are described later.)

To contour the body, draw midlines down the centers of the sides, front and back. These serve as reference points when you contour the body from high to low points. For this step, use either file or plane—or both. Finally, dress any convex areas with the shaver.

Finishing is a matter of personal preference, but it is dictated somewhat by both subject matter and type of wood. The owl was sanded smooth, then stained and varnished. Other subjects, in softwoods, are better finished with a textured surface. The crocodile illustrated on page 133, for example, was rough textured with a coarse wire brush chucked into a portable drill. Its finish is a black flat enamel, followed by two coats of a semigloss varnish.

About those Surform (pronounced *sirform*) tools: There are several reasons why they will quickly be among your favorites. One of the best reasons is the good control of the tool the user has. Even a beginner will soon be able to remove just the right amount of stock—no more, no less —from where he wants it removed. A scarlike gash in a piece of wood (a common mishap with a gouge in the hands of one unfamiliar with woodgrains) is virtually impossible with a Surform tool.

Carpenters have used these tools since they came on the scene in 1956. Professional sculptors, arts and crafts teachers and hobbyists quickly followed suit when they learned the tools could be used to work wood, stone and metals. Homeowners soon discovered how handy the tools are for household jobs.

The tools are not expensive, need no adjustments and you need not be a sharpening expert either. The long-lasting blades are simply dis-carded when worn. Replacement blades fall within the $1 to $2.25 price range. The tools are safe, too. Youngsters and beginners can use them because they are virtually accidentproof.

Manufactured by Stanley Tools, 195 Lake St., New Britain, Conn. 06050, Surform tools are sold in hardware outlets throughout the United States. Until now, there were five tools in the line. About to be introduced are two new versions. All seven have been tested by *PM*.

In the photo on page 136, you see the **mini-file** and **shaver**. Both have been shop-tested by several *PM* editors. Opinions were unanimous that the tools are welcome additions to this versatile line. The first lets you plane right up to a vertical member that butts horizontal—a decided advantage in cabinetmaking. The shaver greatly simplifies the shaping of convex curves— by pulling rather than pushing action. It also does a fine job of smoothing end grain and plywood edges.

other Surform tools

File-type tool. It cuts faster than a metal file or wood rasp. As on all Surform tools, the blade is nonclogging and the tool provides maximum user comfort.

Round file. It has the same characteristics as the above tool. Primarily, it's used to enlarge holes and for smoothing curved, concave surfaces.

Plane-type tool. The body has integral front and rear grip handles, and the tool feels particularly comfortable in your hand. The 450 teeth assure maximum cutting action with minimum effort.

Pocket tool. It is worked in much the same manner as an ordinary block plane. The tool is designed to fit the palm comfortably, with complete control when you shave hard-to-reach spots.

Drum tool. Since it's designed for use with power (chucked in a drill press, ¼-in. or larger portable drill, or with a flexible shaft) it's not for youngsters. Using the drum requires experience. The spinning drum, as can be expected, removes stock rapidly and is safe in the hands of a competent operator.

I found that it is important to feed the work as shown in the sketch, page 134. Start around the midpoint of the workpiece and trail the work through. *Never* feed the lead edge into the revolving cylinder.

BY WAYNE C. LECKEY

From bottles to fancy glassware

There is no end to the things you
can make from bottles with the new
bottle and jug cutters

■ THERE IS SOMETHING UNIVERSAL in the appeal of an attractive, fancy bottle—its color, size, and shape—and for years people have tried to make things from bottles. The big bugaboo was cutting them. Many makeshift and primitive methods were used, including the old trick of soaking a string in kerosene, tying it around the bottle, igniting the string and then plunging the bottle in water to fracture it at the string. There was no guarantee the method would work, and seldom did you wind up with a clean, even break.

new cutting equipment

The current bottle-cutting craze has changed all that. Now simple cutting equipment available in kits has taken all the guesswork out of cutting a bottle. It's so simple you can make a clean, even cut every time. Wine and beer bottles, even large glass jugs, which were normally thrown away, are being converted into all kinds of attractive and useful pieces of glassware such as you see displayed here. Tall wine bottles make graceful bud vases when the tops are cut off and cemented to shallow sections of the bottoms. A gallon jug cut near the top and then cemented to a base cut from a quart bottle becomes a pretty fruit bowl. The bottom part of the jug will serve as a candy dish when cut 2 in. deep. The lower half of a straight-sided liquor bottle makes a perfect hurricane lamp when fitted with a stubby candle. Ashtrays for the patio or porch can be made from the bottoms of bottles. The possibilities are practically endless.

Beer bottles make good practice bottles as they cut and polish easily. Wine bottles offer an interesting range of shapes, colors and sizes. The glass is of better quality than beer bottles and thicker. Burgundy, Bordeaux or champagne bottles, which have dimpled bottoms, make extra-attractive pieces.

Basically, there are two types of bottle-cutting kits on the market: One cuts the bottle vertically,

The Stylecraft kit includes a bottle cutter, candle, strips of coarse-grade and fine-grade silicone-carbide paper and a vial of carbide grits. The candle is used to heat the etch. The glass is then cracked with an ice cube. The paper and grit are used to grind and polish the cut edge

the other, horizontally. The vertical cutter uses the top of the bottle as a guide to swing the glass cutter around the outside of the bottle. The horizontal cutter uses the bottom of the bottle as a guide, the glass cutter remains stationary and the scoring is done by rotating the bottle around the cutter.

Of the two methods, I found the horizontal one the easier. You don't have to go through a lot of adjusting and fussing to cut bottles of different diameters; you just cradle the bottle against a stop and turn it. Once the stop is set for height, you can't miss when making matched sets of glasses—all will be of uniform size. I also found there is less waste. If two sections don't break cleanly when you're using a horizontal cutter, you can continue to salvage the base of the bottle since you don't need the neck to re-cut it.

Ephren's Old Time Bottle Cutter Kit by Stylecraft (shown here) cuts the bottle in a horizontal position. It sells for about $10 at stationery stores or by mail from Stylecraft, 1800 Johnson St., Baltimore, Md. 21230.

● **Cutting.** The key to successful bottle cutting is the scoring. Only a *light etch should be made, and only one time around the bottle.* It is important that the adjustable cutting wheel always be at a right angle to the glass surface to assure a straight cut and a flat edge. It's also important to put a drop of oil on the cutter each time you cut a bottle.

To score a bottle, remove the label and place the bottle in the cradle on the rollers with the bottom against the backstop. Grip the bottle with both hands as shown and with a constant, even pressure, turn the bottle toward you without stopping. A jerky motion will cause the cutter to skip and make an uneven etch. A slight crunching sound will signal one time around the bottle and when you hear it, stop. Avoid retracing the original score as this will chip the glass and damage the cutter. To assure perfect alignment of the etch from beginning to end, it is important

1. The bottle is cut by placing it on the cutter rollers and rotating it one turn to etch the glass lightly

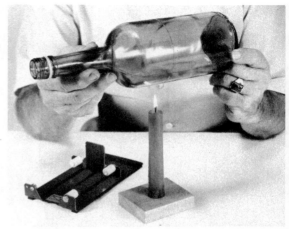

2. The etched line is heated by holding the bottle over the candle flame and rotating it two or three times

3. The glass is cracked neatly along the etched line by chilling the heated glass with an ice cube

4. The edge is polished by dipping it in water and rubbing on a flat surface sprinkled with carbide grit

to keep the bottom of the bottle in contact with the backstop as you turn it.

● **Heating.** To separate the bottle at the etched line you first heat the line with a candle. Hold the bottle horizontally over the candle about ¼ in. away from the tip of the flame, and slowly rotate it three or four times in one direction. Then turn it three or four more times at a faster pace. The glass should feel hot to the touch, but not too hot to handle.

● **Cooling.** Now place the bottle in an upright position and, before the bottle cools, rub an ice cube around the etched line several times until the etch becomes a crack. If the etched line has been properly heated, a crack will start to form the instant the ice touches the glass and will continue around the bottle as it is chilled by the ice,

resulting in a comparatively smooth fracture. The smoothness of the edge is very important because the grinding of the edge is the hardest part of bottle-cutting.

If the two sections fail to part with a slight tug, don't force them; reheat the etch and try again. Sometimes it's necessary to repeat the heating and cooling steps several times depending on the thickness of the glass. More times than not, the bottle will pop apart cleanly.

● **Polishing.** The final step is polishing the cut edge. This is done by first rubbing the inside and outside edges lightly with the coarse carborundum paper. Then carbide grit is sprinkled on a flat, hard surface such as a piece of window glass. The cut bottle is dipped in water and placed on the polishing surface. Start to grind in a circular motion. After a short time (10 to 15 minutes, depending on the thickness of the glass) the edge will become perfectly flat and take on a "frosted" appearance. While you're grinding, keep the rim of the glass wet at all times—the water will make the grinding action more effective. Sprinkle the carbide grit in a circle rather than concentrate it in one spot. Now you are ready to round the sharp edges with the fine-grit paper, dipping it in water as you rub.

● **Cementing.** Epoxy adhesive (I used Scotch Epoxy Adhesive, 3M Co.) is used to cement the top of one bottle to the bottom of another. Mix a small amount of the two-part cement and apply it sparingly. Support the work in an upright position and set aside overnight for the cement to harden. Finally, polish your finished piece with glass wax.

These are typical wine, beer and liquor bottles you can turn into handsome and useful pieces of glassware

A sofa for less than $100

For young homemakers here is a sofa which is
well-designed, easy-to-build, and sturdy

BY WINSTON S. GOO

■ IF YOUR WIFE wants to help you build this
modern sofa, you can put her to work sewing the
cushions while you take on the construction. Together you can make it for less than $100, which
is about $200 less than what it would cost you in
a store.

You can make it a chummy 78 in. long, or a
king-size 90 in. The latter size will cost about
$35 for plywood and clear pine, $3 for hardware
and $3 more for wood stain. The cushions will
run about $32 for top-grade foam and another
$25 for fabric. If your wife is not handy with
needle and thread, add another $20 for sewing.

As you'll see after studying the drawing, it is
a simple thing to build. Its boxlike construction
requires the better part of three full sheets of
plywood, two ¾ in. thick and one ⅜ in.

Both arms are made alike except for being
right and left-hand assemblies. The 8 and 10-ft.
lengths of clear 1x4 are used for the fronts and
tops of the arms, the top of the back and apron
along the front.

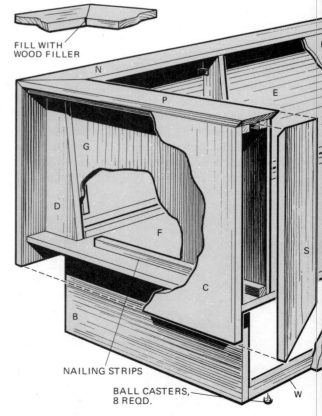

FILL WITH
WOOD FILLER

NAILING STRIPS

BALL CASTERS,
8 REQD.

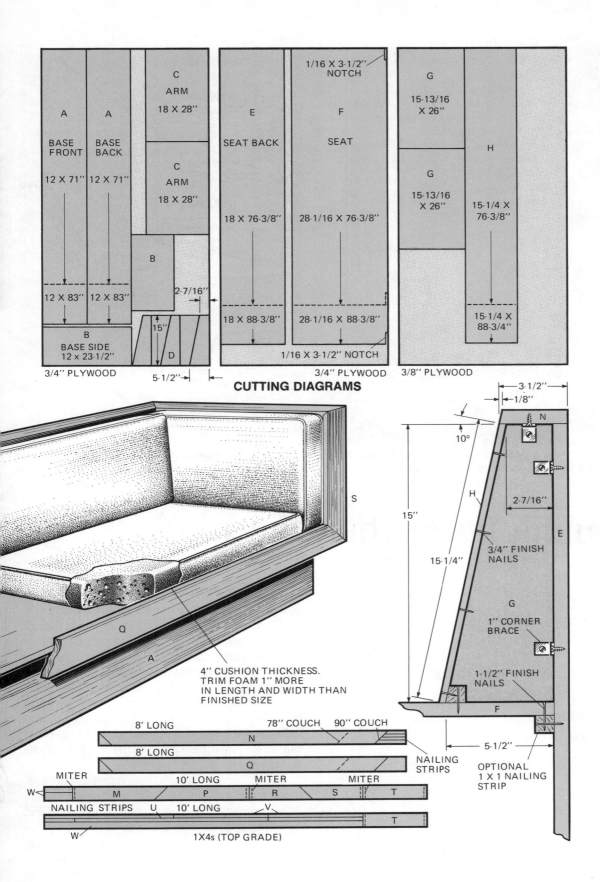

C
ARM
18 X 28"

A
BASE FRONT
12 X 71"

A
BASE BACK
12 X 71"

C
ARM
18 X 28"

B

12 X 83"   12 X 83"

2-7/16"

15"

B
BASE SIDE
12 x 23-1/2"

D

3/4" PLYWOOD

5-1/2"

1/16 X 3-1/2"
NOTCH

E
SEAT BACK

F
SEAT

18 X 76-3/8"

28-1/16 X 76-3/8"

18 X 88-3/8"

28-1/16 X 88-3/8"

1/16 X 3-1/2" NOTCH

3/4" PLYWOOD

G
15-13/16
X 26"

H

G
15-13/16
X 26"

15-1/4 X
76-3/8"

15-1/4 X
88-3/4"

3/8" PLYWOOD

CUTTING DIAGRAMS

S

Q

A

4" CUSHION THICKNESS.
TRIM FOAM 1" MORE
IN LENGTH AND WIDTH THAN
FINISHED SIZE

3-1/2"
1/8"

N

10°

H

15"

15-1/4"

2-7/16"

3/4" FINISH
NAILS

E

G

1" CORNER
BRACE

1-1/2" FINISH
NAILS

F

5-1/2"

OPTIONAL
1 X 1 NAILING
STRIP

8' LONG   78" COUCH   90" COUCH

N

8' LONG

Q

NAILING
STRIPS

MITER

W

M   10' LONG   MITER   MITER

P   R   S   T

NAILING STRIPS   U   10' LONG   V

T

W

1X4s (TOP GRADE)

143

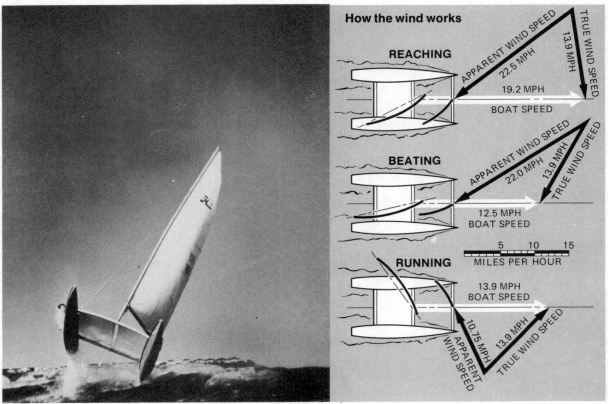

How the wind works

REACHING

APPARENT WIND SPEED 22.5 MPH

TRUE WIND SPEED 13.9 MPH

19.2 MPH
BOAT SPEED

BEATING

APPARENT WIND SPEED 22.0 MPH

TRUE WIND SPEED 13.9 MPH

12.5 MPH
BOAT SPEED

5   10   15
MILES PER HOUR

RUNNING

13.9 MPH
BOAT SPEED

10.75 MPH APPARENT WIND SPEED

13.9 MPH TRUE WIND SPEED

Hobie Cat, from Coast Catamaran, San Juan Capistrano, Calif. has been officially clocked at an incredible 26 mph

Broad reach gives racing catamaran the highest speed. The vector drawings above show how it is done with this craft

Sailing faster than the wind

BY N. M. IYE

Incredible as it may seem,
efficient sails and multihulls
make some boats swifter than
the mighty breezes that push them
through the water or over the ice

■ SAILING FASTER than the wind seems impossible—like getting something for nothing.

Yet thousands of boats can do this, though most skippers do not fully understand why or how. Iceboats can sail about four times the speed of the wind that drives them. Racing catamarans can do about 1.2 times the speed of the wind, and future multihull designs may get up to twice the speed of the wind. Some planing monohulls can go faster than the wind. But keel boats can never equal the speed of the wind, let alone go faster.

There is a general misunderstanding that sailboats move only because the moving air pushes them downwind. It seems illogical that an object could move faster than the force moving it.

That was true in the days of old square-riggers and before man learned to sail into the wind. But now the answer involves the difference between the true velocity and the apparent wind velocity.

Hiking out on one hull of a swift *Hobie Cat* in a brisk wind is the designer of the boat, Hobie Alter

True wind seems obvious enough. It is simply the speed of air passing a fixed point. It may shift around a bit, but it usually has a general direction or heading.

Apparent wind is something else. Suppose you are walking or running. On a calm day you will feel the wind directly in front of you. But suppose there is a 10-mile wind blowing from your right. As you run forward at about 5 mph, you will feel the apparent wind shift to the right front quarter of your face. You know the wind is still coming from the right, but adding in your forward speed makes the apparent wind shift up ahead—so it comes in from a forward, as well as side, angle. If you increase your forward speed and the side wind stays the same, the apparent wind shifts even farther ahead.

This is what happens with a boat. With an iceboat the runners traveling over a hard, slick surface meet little resistance going forward. With a sailboat the hull must displace water that is heavy and also meet friction resistance caused by its wetted surface. Keeping the boat light makes it possible for a boat to move faster. Keelboats are weighty, so they displace equally large weights of water and put up substantial frontal area resistance as well. The combination makes it impossible to outspeed the wind.

But with lightweight, highly-streamlined catamarans the story is different. Since the hulls skim the surface, the faster they go the faster the ap-parent wind becomes. Even when going downwind, iceboats and racing catamarans tack from side to side to get the most speed from the apparent wind. The result: Even though the total distance from side to side is much greater than the straight-line distance downwind, they can cover the straight-line distance in less time than if they merely drifted.

As diagrams on page 144 indicate, the highest apparent winds are achieved on a broad reach, and as the speed builds up and the apparent wind moves forward, the fastest heading of the boat moves away from the true wind. At its highest speed the boat is actually going away from the true wind but still into the apparent wind. All the time the angle of the boat to the apparent wind stays almost the same, no matter what the course is in relation to the true wind. The angle of an iceboat may be 10° to 20° off the apparent wind.

More exciting are relative speeds. For an iceboat, speeds up to 50 or 60 mph are possible with winds of only 15 mph. On a conventional sailboat, speeds to 6 mph are possible with 10-mph winds. High-performance catamarans have reached 35-mph speeds with 25-mph winds.

This last figure points up the drag of water friction that holds a sailboat back. Possibly when hydrofoils and more advanced sails are developed, the relative speeds of waterborne boats will approach the almost dragless efficiency of iceboats.

Carrying a standard load, a boat approaches the first marker (foreground) of the timing trap

How fast does your boat really go?

BY JIM MARTENHOFF

■ HERE'S A SPEEDY boat-speed trick that works on any lake, bay, river or stream. You set up your own speed trap, and do it in a way that makes the arithmetic extra easy. You can check out your speedometer or get quick miles-per-hour without one, determine boat performance and calibrate a tachometer to read your boat speeds as well.

We'll be talking statute miles exclusively (most small-craft owners do since it makes their rigs seem faster than nautical-mile speeds do), but instead of calling a mile 5280 feet long we'll call it 3600 seconds, the number of seconds in an hour.

Run a measured mile. Time your boat in seconds. Divide seconds run into 3600 and the answer is your speed. If you run the mile in 100 seconds, you're going 36 miles an hour. It's that

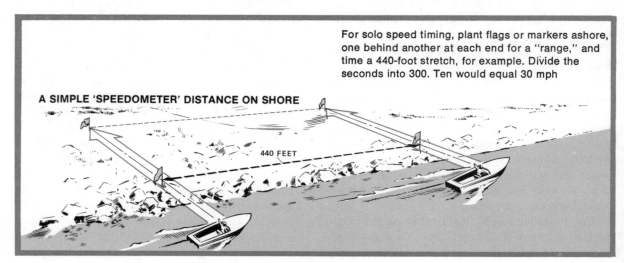

For solo speed timing, plant flags or markers ashore, one behind another at each end for a "range," and time a 440-foot stretch, for example. Divide the seconds into 300. Ten would equal 30 mph

A SIMPLE 'SPEEDOMETER' DISTANCE ON SHORE

440 FEET

simple and a lot less work than any of the time-speed-distance formulae that can be found in textbooks.

If a mile is 3600 seconds, then a half-mile is 1800, a quarter mile is 900 and so on. Measure off a distance of 440 feet which equals 300 seconds, run the trap, and if your time is 10 seconds your speed is 30 mph.

Your trap is measured along any handy beach or stretch of shoreline where you can run parallel to it, within easy sight of your markers. Make sure there are no shoals or rocks. Any respectable distance between easy-to-spot trees, boulders or other landmarks will work. If they don't stand out enough, a dab of paint can mark them. Stakes at right angles between them and the water can provide "ranges" for sighting.

A 100-foot tape measure will make trap measuring easy, but you can also use a measured length of 50 or 100 feet of anchor or ski-tow line plus a short tape. Laying out your trap makes a good boat club project.

When you have your trap length measured in feet, you convert it to "seconds" to simplify that math. To do this, multiply your trap length by .682 (a conversion factor derived by dividing 5280 into 3600). A seven-place answer is .6818-181, but rounded off to three is plenty. Again, you only multiply trap length times .682 once. Then you can forget the foot-length of your trap and just remember the length in terms of time.

Suppose you measure between two trees and find they are 565 feet apart. Multiplying by .682 gives 385.33 which you can round off to 385. Run your distance and time it. You'll need a stopwatch. You can round off long distances but you can't round off running times. Suppose you ran that 385-trap in 13.3 seconds. Divide 385 by 13.3 and your speed comes out to 28.9 statute miles per hour. To cancel out any wind or currents, run your trap both ways.

Don't worry about timing-lag errors as you punch the stopwatch. They tend to cancel out after several runs. To improve accuracy, sight across a windshield brace, seatback or even the top of the motor. Start and stop the watch when your range ashore lines up with your sighting line fixture aboard. Carrying an observer aboard to do this makes driving easier, and to determine useful speeds you should load up first with the passengers and even the ice, drinks, gas and gear that you normally carry.

For determining true speeds at a variety of throttle settings, the simple division calculations

Lining up the boat windshield with in-line dockside landmarks provides accurate start and finish points for the speed trap. Boat clubs can also station timers ashore at each end of the measured course to clock and record up and downwind passes by member drivers

A tape-measure check of the distance between the trap markers is a tedious job, but once it is completed, it can provide a permanent course for boating speed checks

time your boat, continued

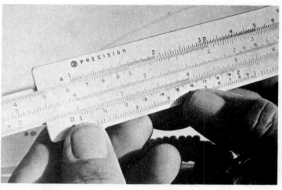

Calculations must be based on stopwatch timing (seconds cannot be rounded off), but a slide rule, shown here indicating 25 mph for a 440-foot range, makes figuring quick and easy. The speeds resulting can be pasted around the tach to convert it into a speedometer

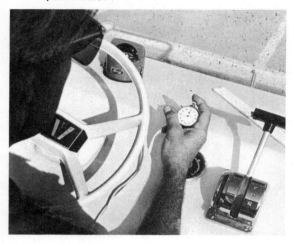

can be made with pencil and paper, even though this is admittedly tedious.

For an easier way to do this, just buy or borrow one of the popular new little pocket-sized electronic calculators. Or try a dime-store substitute—a plastic slide rule. Use the "C" and "D" scales along the bottom. As shown in our illustration, we had a trap 440 feet long which converts to 300 seconds. Running time was 12 seconds, and the mark for 12 on the "D" scale was placed directly under the 3 on the "C" scale, which stands for 300 seconds. (The only knack to using a slide rule is learning to insert your own zeros and decimals.) You read the answer directly above the 1 on the "D" scale—in this case, 25 miles per hour.

Slide rules come with simple directions, and as you can see, it takes only a few moments to compute speeds and it doesn't matter if your time is in fifths or tenths of a second.

Once you know your top speed, what next? Make at least two more runs, one at bare planing speed and another at moderate cruising speed. If you think you'll ever need it, make timed runs with the boat off plane at speeds such as you might use in nasty going during poor weather. Write down these speeds while noting the readings on the tachometer, which most speedy outboards and stern drives have. On dime-store graph paper, write the rpm down the left side in units of 100 or 200, and write speeds across the bottom the same way. Plot your timed speeds on the graph opposite your recorded rpm numbers and connect your marks into a curve.

Now you have a table of speeds for various rpm settings. Yachtsmen might carry this around in a log book, which can be a pain in the neck in a small boat. Instead, use this trick. Pick suitable speeds for slow cruise, fast cruise, ski speed perhaps, and wide open. With a labelmaker, print these speeds, cut them with an arrow-point and paste them at proper rpm spots around the rim of your tach to make it into a speedometer. It will prove to be accurate enough for small-boat open-water navigation.

When using charts and nautical miles, multiply statute speeds by .8689 and they become knots —which are nautical miles per hour.

Sounds like a lot of work? Not really. You only measure your speed trap once, and many of your calculations, once figured, are good until you change hull or engine.

Spectacular ski tricks you can learn

BY HARRIS E. DARK

■ SPEEDING ALONG on slats over the water is probably one of the safest of all outdoor sports —even if you try such spectacular tricks as skiing backwards, jumping wakes or holding onto the ski rope with your toes.

That's the word from vivacious, 20-year-old Christie Freeman of Thayer, Mo., champion trick and slalom skier, who's been skiing since she was 5.

If you're doubtful that you can learn anything

World's champion gold medalist
Christie Freeman shows you how to
do some of her advanced ski routines

Skier's salute is an early exercise for practice on one ski

Two-ski side slide uses the trick skis without bottom fins

Leg tow is an easy trick and good exercise for balance

about trick skiing from words and pictures, just look at Christie. She picked up most of the basic tricks from publications of the American Water Ski Assn.—until she took second place in her first contest at age 12. Tournaments and titles have followed, and at 18 last year Christie took first place in tricks and set a new world female record in slalom at the California International Cup tournament, only to break her own record twice and win the Women's World Slalom Gold Medal at the World Water Ski Championships in Spain. Not too bad, just from learning a few basic skills by studying some words and pictures!

A beginning skier, Christie advises, should fit on his skis ashore first to learn using the legs to

Dock start must be prepared for by carefully coiling the line so it feeds freely on "hit it" command

stand while keeping back and arms straight. Practicing the deep-water start, seated back on the skis with knees to chest and ski tips up, comes next. Once you have skied, zigzagged across the wake of the towboat (and fallen) enough to feel at ease and secure on your skies, why not try some advanced maneuvers?

● **The skier's salute,** with one ski raised from the water and almost vertical to it, is your introduction to one-ski tricks and slalom. With knees slightly bent to act as shock absorbers and weight well back, your lift foot is arched to keep the forward tip of your ski well up and your knee raised toward your chest. Any dip of the ski tip can trip you or pull off the ski.

Once you can lift one ski easily, ride on it and practice lifting the other until you are equally at ease on either foot. Again, practice ashore before trying it on the water. Eventually, Christie points out, you will find one foot which feels more comfortable for advanced one-ski tricks. Slalom and tricks require development of real strength in both legs, however, so she recommends alternate left and right practice.

● **Two-ski side slide** is the basis for a number of more complicated turns. Trick skis are necessary, with no fin on the bottom. They are usually shorter and more rounded than beginners' skis. At between 15 and 20 mph, take a slightly crouching position with arms partially bent. As the tow handle is pulled in, turn body in direction of the turn. Outside ski comes around and in front of inside ski while inside hand releases grip on tow handle; the inside shoulder is lowered slightly while skis have small slope away from the towboat and are wide enough apart for firm

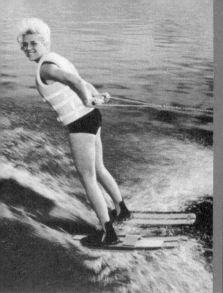

Backward on two is first tried
on flat, then across the wakes

Single ski backward takes
more lean, with weight forward

Toe-tow on one requires exact
balance and much practice

stance. To return to forward skiing, waist-high handle is moved out from inline with feet toward ski tips as body turns skis to point ahead again.

● **Front-to-back turn** is a continuation of the side slide but through 180°. With the handle pulled in waist-high toward the body in a partial crouch, the skier turns and reaches behind his back to grab tow handle with hand on inside of turn as the outside ski comes around. Skis are kept farther apart for better balance until reverse tracking position is reached. While traveling backward, the skier leans away from the pull of the tow rope, keeps knees slightly bent, and holds tow handle in middle of back with arms bent to absorb tow shock. Procedure is reversed to return to forward skiing position.

Skiing backward can commence from a deep-water start. With towboat in gear and moving forward fast enough to keep towline taut, the skier turns in the water so that he faces away from boat with rear ski tips above the surface and towline held with both hands behind hips. To signal for the boat to accelerate, the skier drops his head under water while lowering hand-grip level with his heels. Skier must straighten up from crouch slowly after boat speed lifts him into skiing position.

● **One-ski tricks** require some of the same turning techniques as with two, but with a different balance. About 60 percent of body weight will be on the rear foot while the skier travels forward. Running backward, however, it is necessary to place 75 percent of body weight on the forward foot away from the towboat and to lean

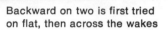

Rear-view mirror is now required by law in some states. It must give driver view of skier

well forward toward the front tip of the backward-running ski. Slower tow speeds, down to about 15 mph with light skiers, make balance easier, but the full weight on one ski causes it to track in a deeper groove. For the quick turns which tricks require, the skier will drop smoothly into a deeper crouch, pull in on the tow handle, and then spring up and turn, all in one continuous motion while shifting weight as necessary. A lot of practice is necessary, of course, but the rewards come when you can perform one-ski side slide, front-to-back turn and one-ski 360° turns as easily as you did on two skis.

● **Wake turns** can be your next challenge if you haven't tried them already. Shortening your 75-foot line to about 50 feet will bring you closer to the wake of your towboat. You will really get the sensation of faster movement. Now you will be doing your turns more quickly and in the air as you leap from the lip of the wake. The back-to-front wake turn provides an added problem since you cannot see the wake coming and must time your leap as you feel the slope of the wake from your skis. For one-ski wake turns a left-footed skier will usually cut for the left wake and make a left turn, while the skier with right foot forward will turn right.

The full 360° wake turn is usually started from

Advanced tricks like one-ski slide, toe hold and forward and reverse step-overs can be performed with flotation jacket or belt in tow boat but should always be practiced with preserver worn. Below, Christie gives her driver-brother Pat final instructions on speeds and tricks scheduled before she takes a run off the photo stadium, Cypress Gardens, Florida

One-ski side slide

Toe-hold tow

Front-to-back stepover

Back-to-front stepover

outside the wake. The skier cuts in with the tow-line partially wrapped around him as one hand grips the handle behind the back and the other holds the rope in front until time for the leap, release and turn.

● **Two-ski stepover turns** look simple when Christie performs them but offer an easy opportunity for the beginner to trip himself. Again, practicing ashore with the towline secured is the first step in learning. Expect a few spills when you take to the water and try the hop-up from a crouch, turn and step over to reverse position with the line between the legs all in the same moment. Back-to-front stepover is the reverse procedure. Once again, practice makes perfect.

● **Swan maneuvers** can be attempted with regular tow handles and the heel hooked over the grip for traveling forward or the toes for reverse, but added toe and heel loops or slings are preferable. Swan turns, also known as toehold turns, are a suitable challenge for the advanced skier to perform gracefully, since the arms are not used to ease the strains of the towline and recovery from backward maneuvers requires leg muscles not ordinarily used. For tricks like the 360° swan turn, the skier benefits from the help of an experienced instructor, although even here the beginner can learn much from booklets such as the "ABC's of Trick Skiing," 35 cents from the American Water Ski Assn., Seventh St. and Avenue G, S.W., Winter Haven, Fla. 33880. Memberships and additional instruction pamphlets are available from the organization.

Ski safety includes life jacket, line clear of motors, and alert observer, before heading for jumps

The driver and observer in the towboat are also members of any trick ski performance, Christie Freeman notes, and should know all safety procedures and hand-signal instructions from the skier. To pick up a fallen skier, the driver will circle right if the steering wheel is on the right side of the boat, and will always keep the skier in sight. All safety and pick-up procedures, as well as hand signals, should be reviewed before taking to the water.

HOW TO SIGNAL YOUR DRIVER

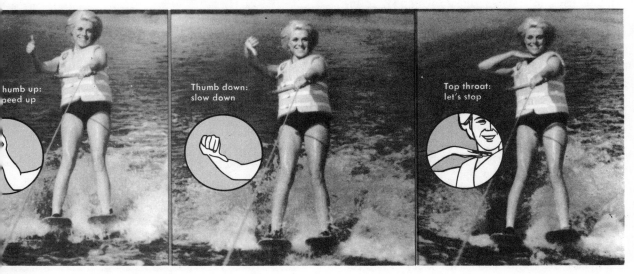

Thumb up: speed up

Thumb down: slow down

Top throat: let's stop

Knots everyone should know

By W. CLYDE LAMMEY

You tie your shoes daily, but
how many other knots do you know?
Here are several that should be
right at your fingertips

■ ROPE, TWINE or cord is of little practical
use unless you knot it to something, around
something, or tie it to itself. Knots usually are
associated with rope or twine, but a good many
other materials can be knotted, such as leather
straps or thongs, fishline, bandages, thread, even
light wire. In fact, anything can be knotted that
is sufficiently flexible to be bent or looped on
itself without breaking.

When tying a knot, think of rope, cord or
twine as having an "end," "bight" and a "standing" part. Think of knots simply as a combination
of three basic turns—the bight, loop and overhand (or underhand). Look closely at the details
at the right and on the following pages and you'll
see how this works out; even in the more involved
knots the basic turns are there in each example.

When rope and cord is in more or less continuous use the ends should be whipped, as indicated, with fine twine or tightly wrapped
thread; or, the ends may be dipped in glue. The
purpose, of course, is to prevent unlaying, or
raveling, of the strands. On a rope of, say, ½ in.
diameter, the whipping should be laid in shellac
or varnish, and should extend at least 1 in. from
the end.

Most of the knots are shown loose—that is, in
the process of being tied; the purpose is to show
the procedure as clearly as possible. In practice,
all knots must be drawn tight before being subjected to stress. Don't trust a knot until it is
drawn up tightly and tested under stress.

As you will notice most knots are designed so
that the parts, or crossings, will bind upon each
other as the stress increases; the harder the pull
the tighter the knot. In some instances the object

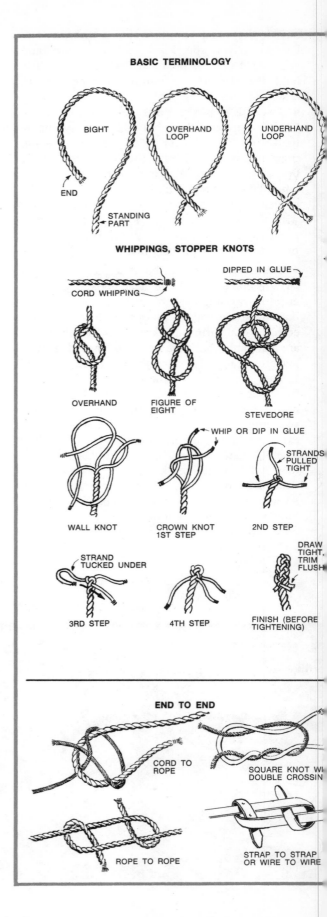

BASIC TERMINOLOGY

BIGHT   OVERHAND LOOP   UNDERHAND LOOP

END

STANDING PART

WHIPPINGS, STOPPER KNOTS

DIPPED IN GLUE

CORD WHIPPING

OVERHAND   FIGURE OF EIGHT   STEVEDORE

WHIP OR DIP IN GLUE

STRANDS PULLED TIGHT

WALL KNOT   CROWN KNOT 1ST STEP   2ND STEP

STRAND TUCKED UNDER

DRAW TIGHT, TRIM FLUSH

3RD STEP   4TH STEP   FINISH (BEFORE TIGHTENING)

END TO END

CORD TO ROPE

SQUARE KNOT WI DOUBLE CROSSIN

ROPE TO ROPE   STRAP TO STRAP OR WIRE TO WIRE

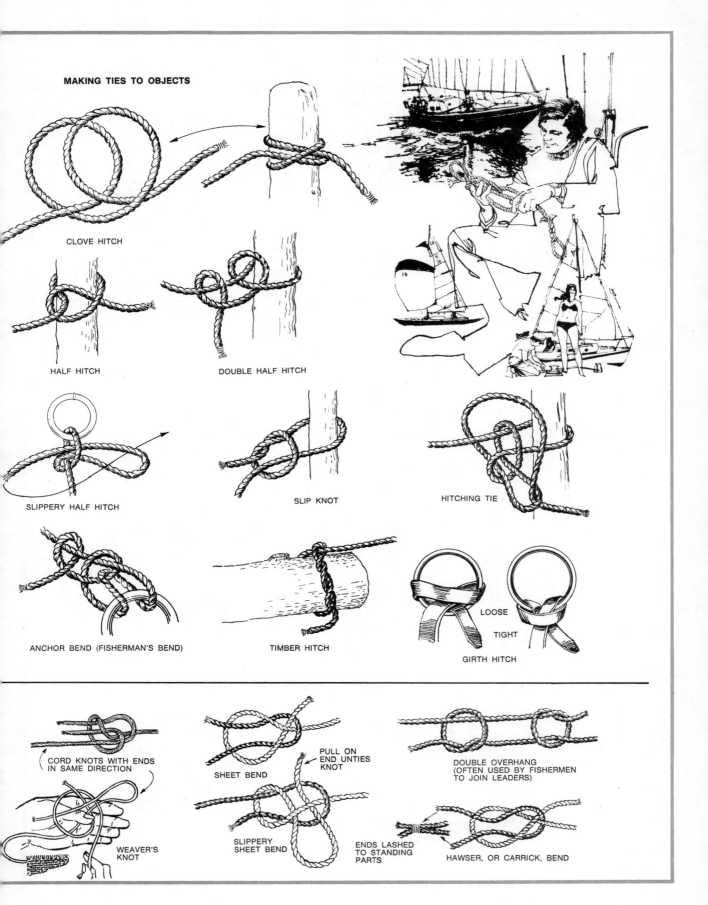

MAKING TIES TO OBJECTS

CLOVE HITCH

HALF HITCH

DOUBLE HALF HITCH

SLIPPERY HALF HITCH

SLIP KNOT

HITCHING TIE

ANCHOR BEND (FISHERMAN'S BEND)

TIMBER HITCH

LOOSE

TIGHT

GIRTH HITCH

CORD KNOTS WITH ENDS
IN SAME DIRECTION

SHEET BEND

PULL ON
END UNTIES
KNOT

DOUBLE OVERHANG
(OFTEN USED BY FISHERMEN
TO JOIN LEADERS)

WEAVER'S
KNOT

SLIPPERY
SHEET BEND

ENDS LASHED
TO STANDING
PARTS

HAWSER, OR CARRICK, BEND

155

tied applies the tension necessary to bind the crossings. An example is the sack tie, or miller's knot.

For additional protection, and in some instances purely for ornamental purposes, the ends of a length of rope may be knotted. Typical are the wall knot and the crown knot detailed on page 154. Note that these are more in the nature of splices than are the common knots and hitches designed for joining rope or cord to objects. The strands are separated and threaded back through the lay as indicated. In the process, the separated strands must be drawn uniformly as the threading, or tucking, proceeds. When threading is finished, the ends of the strands are trimmed flush and the whole rolled between the palms to give a uniform contour.

The single half hitch will hold, given a steady pull on the standing part but may tend to loosen when the stress varies. To assure greater reliability many users tie a "stopper" such as the figure of eight or the stevedore's knot in the end. Other users prefer the double half hitch or perhaps the anchor bend.

Notice that the so-called slippery half hitch can be "locked" by passing the free end through the eye. Otherwise it is easily untied by a pull on the free end. This knot should always be locked if subjected to varying tension. In this it is somewhat similar to the hitching tie. Notice, too, the similarity of the timber hitch, used where it is necessary to tow a log or other long, round object. In some instances the standing part is turned in the direction opposite from that shown, and a second half hitch is made around the object near the end. This tends to steady the log and make towing easier over long distances.

Splicing a rope is quite simple, but it must be done with close attention to procedure as in details A, B and C on the opposite page. When finished, the ends of the strands are trimmed and the splice rolled lightly between the palms or underfoot. The eye splice is handy where it is necessary to hold or exert a steady pull on the rope with the hand. It also is a rather showy example of rope work if done neatly.

Rope and cord that is not used very often should be coiled uniformly and stored in a dry place where temperature and humidity remain fairly constant.

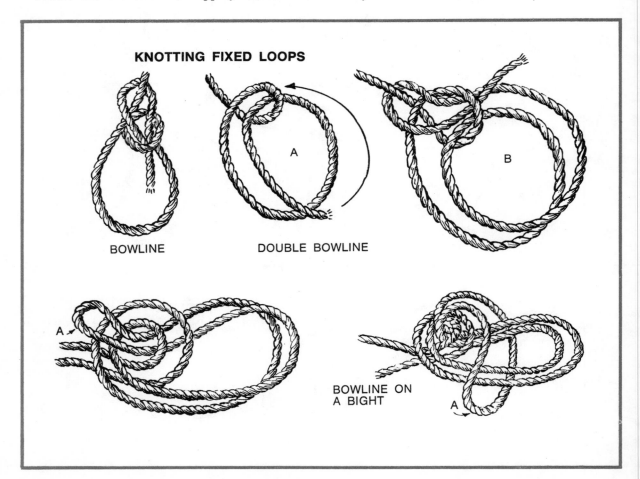

KNOTTING FIXED LOOPS

BOWLINE

A

DOUBLE BOWLINE

B

A

BOWLINE ON A BIGHT

A

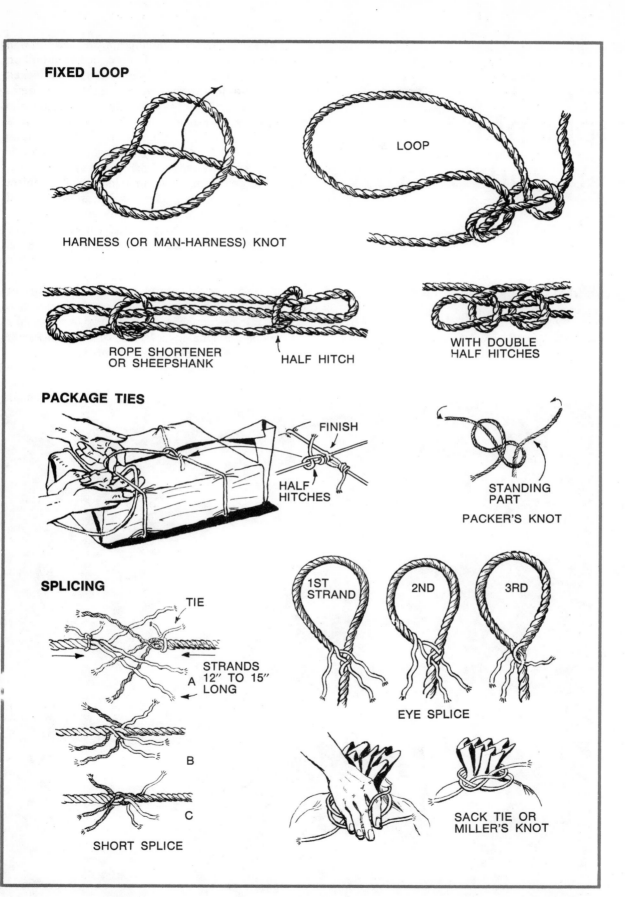

FIXED LOOP

HARNESS (OR MAN-HARNESS) KNOT

LOOP

ROPE SHORTENER
OR SHEEPSHANK

HALF HITCH

WITH DOUBLE
HALF HITCHES

PACKAGE TIES

FINISH

HALF
HITCHES

STANDING
PART

PACKER'S KNOT

SPLICING

TIE

STRANDS
12" TO 15"
LONG

A

B

C

SHORT SPLICE

1ST
STRAND

2ND

3RD

EYE SPLICE

SACK TIE OR
MILLER'S KNOT

Special effects put punch in your pictures

BY BURT MURPHY

Creative, exciting effects are
easy to add to your pictures. All it
takes is practice and the right
accessories, many of which you
can make inexpensively yourself

■ THE FUN IN photography increased when automatic cameras made good, clear photos easy, but automation took some of the fun away, too. You can recapture some of that fun—and dramatize your pictures—with easy (and mostly inexpensive) special effects.

With the right gadgets, a single-lens reflex, and a little know-how, you can:

- Take startling, 180° fisheye views.
- Shoot prismatic, multiple images.
- Vignette away portrait backgrounds.
- Soften portraits with soft focus or diffusion.
- Emphasize distance in scenic shots.

Fisheye shots are less expensive than you may have thought. True, fisheye *lenses* cost hundreds of dollars, but fisheye *attachments* start around $59.95 (for Spiratone and Prinz units) and can fit in front of virtually any lens on any camera.

Fisheye attachments work best on normal or moderate wide-angle lenses, such as a 50 or 35-mm on a 35-mm camera. With very-wide-angle lenses, the circular image may be too small. And

with long telephoto lenses, the curvature of the image is reduced and the effective f-stop becomes uncomfortably slow. Behind-the-lens meters may work with fisheye attachments; if not, or if you're using another type of meter, a ring on the attachment tells the true effective f-stop.

Fisheyes take in more than you may think possible at first. Until you're used to them, you'll find your pictures showing your feet, your tripod's legs or other things you'd rather not have in the picture. Fisheyes distort, but selectively: objects at the picture edge are always curved, but central objects aren't very distorted unless they're very close.

The diaphragm of the prime lens should be wide open when a fisheye attachment is used, and the control ring of the fish-eye should be set to the desired f-stop. For best definition, close down about two to three stops from maximum aperture.

Multiple images require even simpler, less expensive attachments: filter-like prisms designed to produce three, five or six simultaneous images on one frame. Spiratone offers three models: the 3P, which produces three parallel images; the 3C, producing three concentric images, and the 5C that surrounds its central image with four secondary images. Prinz's Mirage is similar, with five secondary images surrounding its central one. Prices, depending on the size and model chosen, range between $9 and $20.

Though these prisms can attach to the front of almost any camera lens, reflex or view cameras are by far the best to use, since they let you place the secondary images exactly where you want them. The prisms also rotate in their mounts, to help you place images precisely; the concentric models may even be rotated during exposure, producing deliberately blurred images surrounding a sharp one.

For more clear-cut images, mount the prism in front of the lens. A paper cup, its inside sprayed with flat black paint, can be used to mount the prism this way.

Multiple images (right) are made with filter-sized prisms mounted in front of your camera lens. Several prism types are available; some give you five concentric images, as in this picture; others give three or four concentric images or three parallel ones. Multiple-image prisms are designed to mount like filters, but can be held an inch or two ahead of the lens. A paper cup, spray-painted black inside, makes such a mount (below); but you'll have to focus and adjust your aperture before you cover the lens with the paper cup

Fisheye shots (left) take in an ultrawide, 180° angle. But unlike the regular wide-angle lenses, they curve the objects in their field of view, with the curvature increasing toward the edge of the picture. (The face, since it's in the picture's center, is less curved by the fisheye effect than it is distorted by proximity to the lens). Fisheye attachments (right) fit almost any lens. They start at about $60. When they are used on wide-angle lenses, they produce full circles. When used with a 50-mm lens, the edge of the circle may be lost

Sparkling stars spread out from lights in night scenes, or from sharp highlights in daylight shots, when you use commercial or homemade star filters. To make one, simply cut a piece of screen to fit your lens hood or filter holders. For eight-pointed stars, use two layers of the screen. Using this simplified method you may lose a little contrast

Multi-image prisms don't affect exposure, but they may cut off the corners of the picture at small apertures. Check this by previewing your pictures with the lens stopped down to the f-stop you're actually shooting at.

Star effects—long streaks or crosses of light surrounding strong highlights in daylight pictures, or light sources in night scenes—can add glitter and sparkle to your shots. You can buy filters to produce these effects, or make your own.

Spiratone has three models available: the Crostar 2P, which extends highlights along a single line, and the 1SQ and 2SQ, which produce crossed highlights. Prinz markets the Cross-Screen, producing an effect like that of the 2SQ. Prices are around $5 to $10, about the same as other filters.

To make your own, use aluminum screen patches (or scraps from discarded screens), either cut to fit your filter holder or simply crimped inside a lens hood. These homemade attachments diffuse the image more than commercial ones do, reduce contrast; and they can't be rotated as easily to orient the starlines where you want them.

If you combine two star attachments at right angles, you'll get eight-pointed stars. The angle between the points will vary if you vary the angle between the grids of the attachments.

Vignetting, or gradually blanking out the edges of a picture, is a time-honored technique to focus attention on a subject by separating it from its background. It's usually done in the darkroom, but it's even easier to do it in your camera—and that way, you can vignette your color slides as well.

For maximum control of your vignetting effects, you can use Spiratone's Vignetar attachment (about $16.00), which is adjustable for sharply or softly defined vignettes. Prinz has a spot filter that is not adjustable, but—at around $6.00—is even less expensive. Or you can make your own by rubbing petroleum jelly around the outer portions of a haze filter; here, the effect will vary with the thickness of the coating and

Soft-focus effect (right) makes old-fashioned-looking portraits, hides blemishes. Shot was made with Spiratone's special Portragon soft-focus 100-mm f/4

Vignetting softens look of pictures and hides distracting backgrounds for another soft, old-fashioned touch. Effects vary with lens used (135-mm above left, 50-mm right) and attachment type. Spiratone's Vignetar attachment (above) is adjustable; homemade, nonadjustable types include frosted cellophane tape of lens hood (right) and clear filter with petroleum jelly on edges

the size of the clear central spot. (You can get a similar effect by applying Scotch Magic cellophane tape to a lens hood.)

Longer lenses will enlarge the center spot and soften the edge of the vignette (too long a lens will integrate the spot and vignette into an overall haze). But smaller f-stops sharpen the edge, so you can juggle focal length and f-stop to get precisely the effect you want.

Diffusion and soft focus are also interesting portrait techniques, which soften the image for a more romantic effect and simultaneously minimize skin blemishes.

Diffusion is the milder of the two effects, gently lowering overall contrast by spreading light from the highlights into the shadows. Diffusion filters are available from Prinz, Spiratone and others for about the cost of ordinary filters. You can also make your own by stretching one or more layers of nylon stocking over a filter holder (use black or black-dyed nylon stockings in your color shots).

In cool weather, you can fog the lens by breathing on it, then shoot at the instant the lens has cleared enough to give you the exact effect you want.

Soft-focus, a stronger effect than diffusion, is usually associated with professional portraiture. It's not the same as incorrect focus, but rather a combination of a sharply focused image with an unsharp image that is formed by the lens's aberrations.

Spiratone's Portragon (about $25) is a 100-mm lens (a good focal length for portraiture) with such aberrations deliberately designed in. Its aperture is fixed at f/4; you control exposure by your choice of shutter speed.

Equivalents of many of these products are available at photo stores. If your local store doesn't have what you want, you can get Spiratone products from Spiratone, Inc., 135–6 Northern Blvd., Flushing, N.Y. 11354, and Prinz products from Bass Camera Co., 179 West Madison St., Chicago, Ill. 60602.

Here is a clever gift idea for a friend or relative. With a minimum amount of equipment almost anyone can make these unique bookends

Personalized bookends

BY ROSARIO CAPOTOSTO

■ PHOTOGRAPHIC bookends will add a novel touch to your bookshelves, particularly when they are cutouts of members of the family or friends. And they're ideal for Christmas gift-giving.

Though children make great subjects, grown-ups can get into the act, too. It is easy to photograph your subject posed in a holding or pushing position, and any background will do because it will be cut out. Pose the person against a wall or other vertical prop to represent the books. This helps to obtain a convincing, natural stance. Enlargements can be single or double weight, glossy or matte; it's not too important. Mounting can be on hardboard or ordinary fir plywood.

For permanence, use contact cement to mount the prints, but avoid lumps or bubbles in cement because they show through on the print surface. A better way to mount the pictures is with dry-mounting tissue.

Standard photo dry-mounting tissue doesn't work too well for mounting pictures on materials

1. Materials and tools used: pictures, plywood, electric iron, scissors, kraft paper, mounting tissue

2. Spot-tack tissue to back of the photo using point of the iron. This will keep pieces from shifting

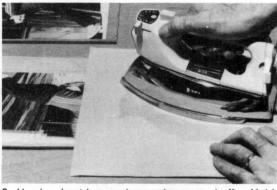

3. Use low-heat iron and wrapping-paper buffer. Hold the paper and slowly pass iron over the "sandwich"

5. Set jigsaw tilting table at a slight angle so the cutout edge bevels slightly to back (i.e., undercut)

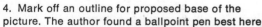

4. Mark off an outline for proposed base of the picture. The author found a ballpoint pen best here

6. Exposed portion of the groove for photo cutout is easily concealed by a glued-in wood spline

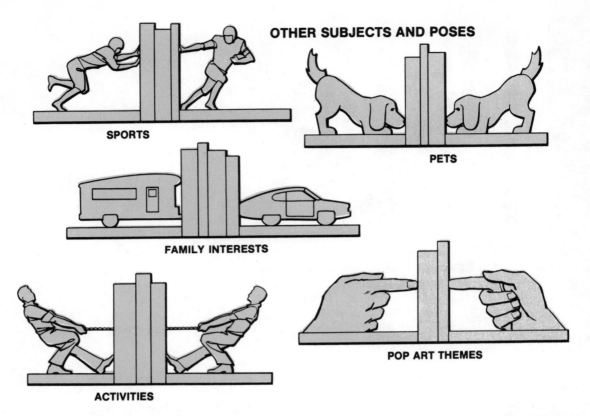

OTHER SUBJECTS AND POSES

SPORTS

PETS

FAMILY INTERESTS

ACTIVITIES

POP ART THEMES

other than cardboard, but there is a special tissue which does. Called Fotoflat, it's made by Seal, Inc., Derby, Conn., and sold at photo and art supply houses. This low-temperature tissue adheres well to wood and requires no special equipment—only an ordinary electric iron.

Set the iron for 180° and pass it over the board and back of the print to preheat. Attach a tissue to the back of the print by spot-tacking it once or twice with the tip of the iron. Tacked spots should be no bigger than ½ in. If the tissue extends beyond the edge of the print, trim it flush. Place the tacked print on the board and cover it with a sheet of clean wrapping paper.

Now apply heat by making a few slow passes with the iron. A total heat time of 5 to 10 seconds for a given area should do. Since the tissue sets while cooling, place the mounting under a flat weight after heating.

If you don't own a power jigsaw, you can make the cutouts by hand with a coping saw. Either way, use a very fine-tooth blade. Before cutting, decide on a suitable design for ending the picture at the bottom and mark this outline on the picture with a ballpoint pen. Also, leave about ¼ in. below the usable part of the picture to serve as a mounting tab which sets into the wood base. (See details below.)

Size and shape of the base is optional but it must have a "tongue" long enough to reach under three or four books to hold properly. Thin galvanized (22-ga.) sheet metal with edges smoothed and felt cloth glued on the bottom serves nicely.

BASE DETAILS

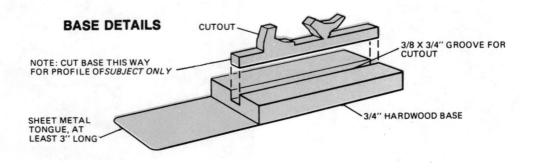

CUTOUT

3/8 X 3/4" GROOVE FOR CUTOUT

NOTE: CUT BASE THIS WAY FOR PROFILE OF *SUBJECT ONLY*

SHEET METAL TONGUE, AT LEAST 3" LONG

3/4" HARDWOOD BASE

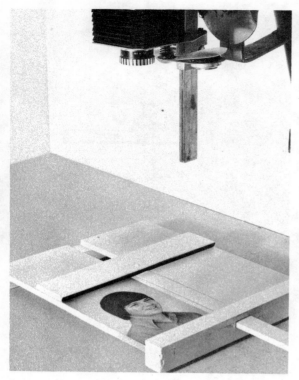

Overhanging bevels on the two stops that contact the enlarging paper hold the paper flat without casting a border shadow onto it. The "T-square" stop slides to adjust for any size of enlarging paper

■ I DON'T LIKE print borders. They're unsightly and they waste paper. So I made this borderless easel in one evening.

The paper's natural curl holds it in place against the overhanging bevels of the two wood stops—but the bevels are so slight that they cast no shadows on the edges of the print.

I made the easel big enough to hold an 8x10 sheet of enlarging paper in either direction, so I can make horizontal or vertical format prints without having to rotate the easel. And I put one of the beveled stops on a sliding "T-square," so it would adjust to hold any paper size.

Dimensions aren't really critical—you can use whatever scrap lumber you have around. But it's important that all pieces be properly squared, both to keep the easel level under the enlarger and to make sure the T-square will slide freely, without binding or chattering. The spring clamp mounts to the bottom of the slider, and rides under the easel platform, providing the tension needed to keep the paper's curl from lifting the sliding stop. I used a 1½-inch speed-nut, with extra holes drilled in it, but any springy metal strip will do if it's longer than the slider slot is wide.

Paint the easel flat white or yellow for easier focusing, and paint the undersides of the bevels black, to prevent reflections.

Borderless enlarging easel

BY LORNE C. BANNISTER

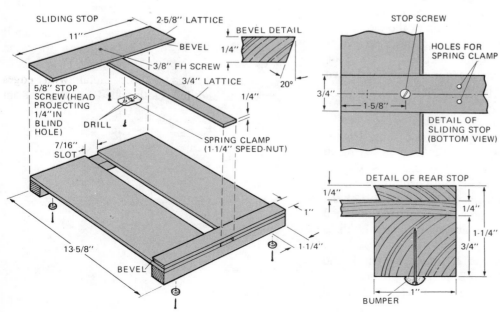

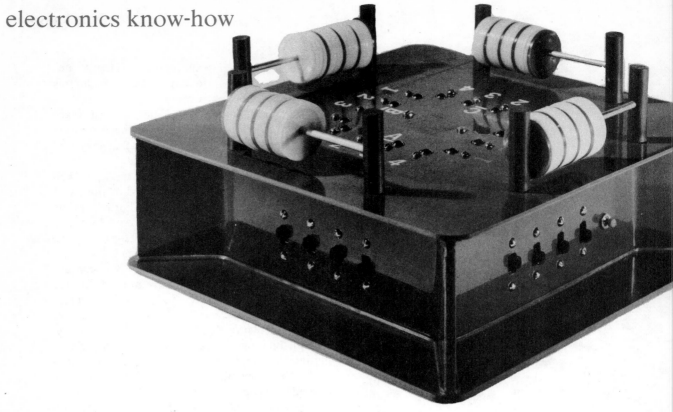

Number-guessing game

BY J. W. CALLENDER

Here's a modern electronic version of a game
you probably played when you were a youngster

■ HERE'S A GAME that really keeps you guessing. It's a modern version of the old fingers game in which the "dealer" (in this case player X) tries to outguess his opponents. It can be played by two, three or four players, and each player has a turn at being player X.

The game is played as follows: Player X, who has the option of pressing either one or two of the four toggle switches in front of him, begins. Then players A, B and C do likewise, trying to guess the number or numbers player X picked. Now player X presses the pushbutton which lights the green and red bulbs on the top of the game to see if an opponent may have matched him. Individual scores are kept by moving discs left to right.

Let's suppose player X presses switch 4, and player A presses 1 and 2, player B presses 2 and 3 and player C presses 3 and 4. Here No. 4 will

An opening in the bottom of the game provides access to batteries and bulbs for replacement

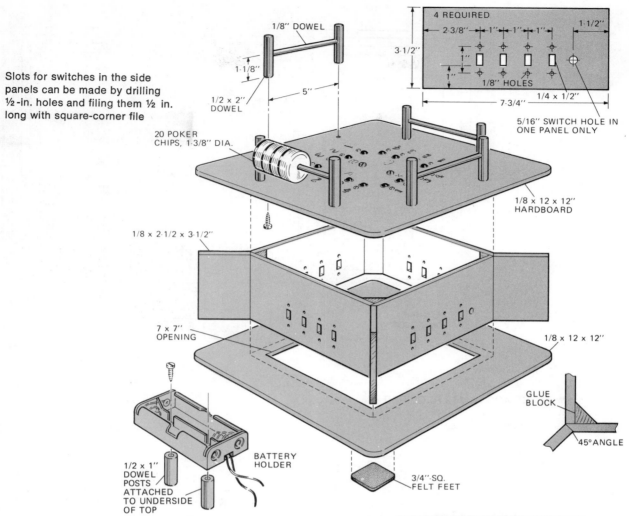

1/8" DOWEL

1-1/8"

5"

1/2 x 2" DOWEL

Slots for switches in the side panels can be made by drilling ½-in. holes and filing them ½ in. long with square-corner file

20 POKER CHIPS, 1-3/8" DIA.

4 REQUIRED

2-3/8" · 1" · 1" · 1"

3-1/2"

1"

1"

1-1/2"

1/8" HOLES

1/4 x 1/2"

7-3/4"

5/16" SWITCH HOLE IN ONE PANEL ONLY

1/8 x 12 x 12" HARDBOARD

1/8 x 2-1/2 x 3-1/2"

7 x 7" OPENING

1/8 x 12 x 12"

GLUE BLOCK

45° ANGLE

1/2 x 1" DOWEL POSTS ATTACHED TO UNDERSIDE OF TOP

BATTERY HOLDER

3/4"-SQ. FELT FEET

light for player C only, allowing him to score one point.

If player A chose 1 and 4, player B, 2 and 4 and player C, 2 and 3, then players A and B would match player X and each score a point.

However, if players A, B and C had all pressed switches 1 and 2, player X would collect a total of three points.

The first player to score 5, 10, 15 or 20 points, whatever number agreed on, wins. All switches are turned off after each guess. Player X has the right to check each player's guess, if he so desires, before he presses the button to turn on the lights. Any combination of numbers may be used by all players.

The scoring discs are 20 poker chips with holes through their centers. Each fifth chip is a different color to make counting easier. All discs are moved to the left before the game begins.

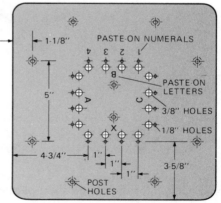

1-1/8"

PASTE-ON NUMERALS

4 3 2 1

B

5"

A

C

PASTE-ON LETTERS

3/8" HOLES

1/8" HOLES

X

4-3/4"

1"

1"

1"

3-5/8"

POST HOLES

The top pattern shows the location of holes used for the lamps, poker-chip racks and battery-holder posts. Each row of holes is numbered

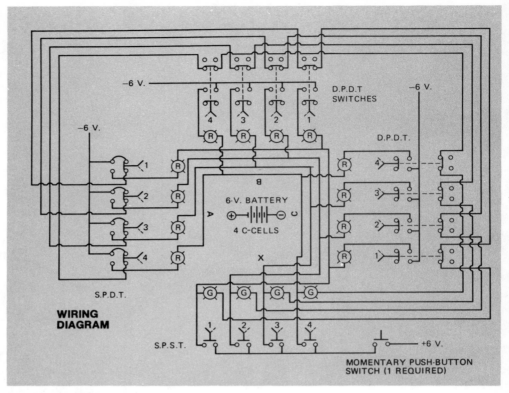

WIRING DIAGRAM

SWITCHES AND LAMPS REQUIRED

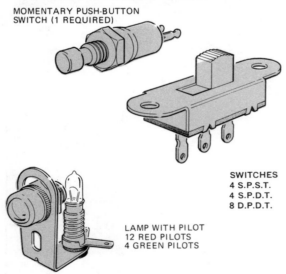

MOMENTARY PUSH-BUTTON
SWITCH (1 REQUIRED)

SWITCHES
4 S.P.S.T.
4 S.P.D.T.
8 D.P.D.T.

LAMP WITH PILOT
12 RED PILOTS
4 GREEN PILOTS

The game can be made of ⅛-in. hardboard and painted, or of colored sheet plastic. Cut four panels 3½ x 7¾ in. and drill and slot them following the pattern. Then bevel one end 45° on the face side. Notice that only one panel is drilled for a pushbutton switch. Glue panels together at the corners to form a box 7⅞ in. square and back up each corner on the inside with a triangular glue block. Finally, glue the 2½ x 3½ in. wings at the four corners.

Now lay out the 12-in.-sq. top panel and drill the ⅜-in. holes for the 16 lamps which fit flush with the surface. The holes in each row are numbered 1, 2, 3 and 4 with paste-on letters, and each row is identified with letters A, B, C and X. Holes are also made in the top for the battery-holder posts, and for the posts which hold the poker chips. Glue the top to the center assembly, but wait until the game is completely wired before gluing the bottom.

You'll need eight double-pole, double-throw (d.p.d.t.), four single-pole, double-throw (s.p.d.t.) and four single-pole, single-throw (s.p.s.t.) switches, plus one momentary push-button switch and 16 miniature pilot lights (4 green and 12 red). All can be purchased at Radio Shack stores. The Philmore battery holder costs around 50 cents. The lights come in packages of three (two red and one green) and sell for about $1.20 per package. The 16 toggle switches cost about $3.65.

Tiny screws (⅜-in. x ⁶⁄₃₂) hold the switches and lights in place. The battery holder for four C-cells is attached to the dowel posts fastened to the underside of the top. Use 20-ga., plastic-covered wire, and solder all connections. Study the wiring diagram carefully before you start.

Don't let brownouts become burnouts

This easily built current checker lets out a loud warning squawk if your line voltage falls below a safe limit

BY RUDOLF F. GRAF and GEORGE J. WHALEN

All's well—meter reads normal line voltage

Whoops! The lights dim, the meter needle falls and the warning beep sounds to indicate a voltage drop (above). The blackout (below) also trips alarm

■ WHEN A BROWNOUT occurs, your lights go dim, the picture on your television screen shrinks, and your electric coffee percolator takes a little longer than usual to perk. You tend to shrug—just the power company cutting back the voltage a bit to conserve juice on a hot day. No harm done. Other things are happening, however, that *can* cause harm.

Induction motors must operate at or near their rated voltage or they're in for trouble. A drop of only 10 percent in line voltage can cause running torque to decrease 19 percent, slip to increase 23 percent, current draw to jump 11 percent and temperature to rise 12° to 15° F. Maximum overload capacity decreases 19 percent. What happens is that the motor, struggling to operate on the reduced voltage, draws excessive current in an attempt to compensate for the loss of power. If the voltage drops too low, intense heat builds up and the motor can burn out. This is an especially serious problem with high-drain appliances such as airconditioners, but it can also affect power tools and other motor-driven home equipment.

While power companies don't intentionally allow line voltages to fall below the safe limit, accidental brownouts can occur. The simple little current checker shown here keeps an eye on your line voltage and automatically beeps a loud warning if it falls below a preset level. It also sounds an alarm if the current goes off altogether, as in a power failure. While a blackout is obvious if it occurs at night when you're awake, it may not be so obvious if you're asleep or if it happens during the day when lights are normally off. The checker alerts you that there's been a

169

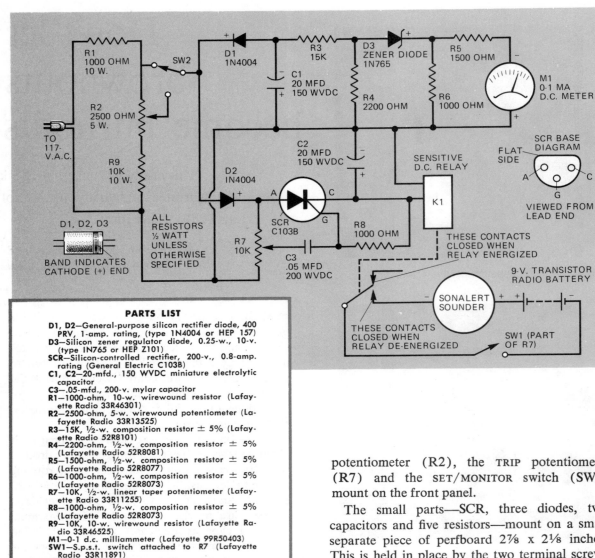

power failure and keeps you from being fooled by clocks that don't tell the right time and morning alarms that don't go off when they should.

The voltage minder is built around a standard 0-1 milliammeter that measures current, a Mallory Sonalert that sounds a high-pitched beep when energized, and a sensing circuit that monitors line voltage and triggers the alarm at a preset point. The parts fit neatly into a 6¼ x 3¾ x 2-inch black Bakelite case. The VOLT ADJUST

potentiometer (R2), the TRIP potentiometer (R7) and the SET/MONITOR switch (SW2) mount on the front panel.

The small parts—SCR, three diodes, two capacitors and five resistors—mount on a small separate piece of perfboard 2⅞ x 2⅛ inches. This is held in place by the two terminal screws on the back of the meter. A conversion scale is needed for the meter so it reads in volts instead of milliamperes. The one shown here is designed to fit standard 3⅛-inch-square panel meters of the type sold by Lafayette Radio. Cut it out and paste it over the existing meter scale, being very careful not to touch the delicate meter needle. Wire the unit as shown in the accompanying diagram. Power resistors (R1 and R9) should be mounted in free space as they get hot and need good ventilation.

To use the checker, simply plug its line cord into any convenient wall outlet. With the SET/MONITOR switch in the MONITOR position (see diagram at SW2), the meter reads a.c. line voltage as it appears at the outlet. To set the checker to the desired trip point, flip the switch to the SET position. This cuts in the VOLT ADJUST potentiometer (R2). Adjust this control until

Parts are mounted in a small black plastic case. While other enclosures can be used, this type is handy because it has a removable front panel of perfboard that can be easily cut and drilled

the meter needle reads the voltage level at which you want the alarm to sound. Since 115 to 120 is normal in most areas, a setting of around 100 volts provides a safe trip point.

With the SET/MONITOR switch still at SET, adjust the TRIP potentiometer (R7) to the point where the Sonalert just goes on, then flip the switch back to MONITOR and leave it there during use. The Sonalert will now go on whenever voltage drops to the preset level. As soon as it does, shut off your airconditioners and other heavy-drain equipment until line voltage returns to normal as indicated by the meter. The Sonalert can be temporarily silenced by turning the TRIP control fully counterclockwise, opening switch SW1. When power returns to normal, reset the TRIP control to its original position. The Sonalert is self-powered by a 9-volt transistor-radio battery so it is independent of house current.

Most of the components are readily available from local radio-parts stores or by mail from Lafayette Radio, 111 Jericho Turnpike, Syosset, N.Y. 11791. If you have difficulty locating the SCR and three diodes, these can be purchased for about $7.50 postpaid from Inventive Electronics, Wykagyl Station, N.Y. 10804.

The small components fit on a separate scrap of perfboard held in place by two terminal screws on the meter. The board is shown tilted up in the photo above before mounting on the meter

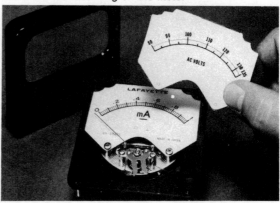

A conversion scale must be added so that the meter reads in volts instead of milliamperes. The one shown below, calibrated from 80 to 135 volts, is actual size and is designed to fit standard 3⅛-inch-square panel meters. Carefully cut it out along the dotted line and cement it over the meter's existing milliampere scale

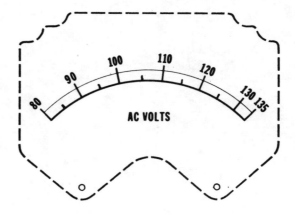

Fit four plastic pontoons under a deck for less than $100, add pint-sized

A tow rig for snorkeling

BY FREDERICK PHILCOX

■ A SIGHTSEEING RIG for skin divers can be a simple project when you use the plastic pontoons available from several sources. Bolt this surface skimmer together and you have a safety raft for divers. Add a little motor and it can tow you on a tour of reefs and underwater sights.

The snorkel-scooter shown here was designed by diving instructor Phil Adams, of Key Colony Beach, Fla., and measurements can be easily altered to fit your special needs. Using more of the pontoons, a raft craft or even houseboat could be constructed for sheltered waters. Cost of the tow rig shown here could come to less

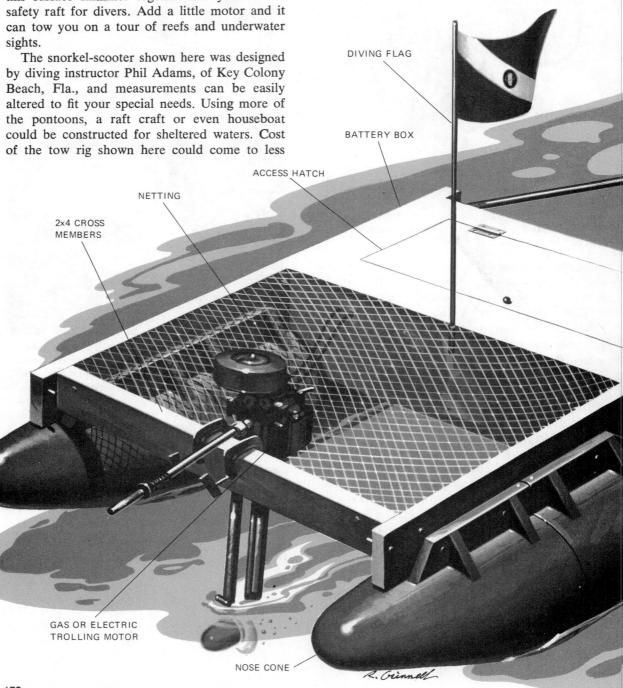

DIVING FLAG

BATTERY BOX

ACCESS HATCH

NETTING

2x4 CROSS MEMBERS

GAS OR ELECTRIC TROLLING MOTOR

NOSE CONE

R. Grinnell

power, and it is a sightseeing skiff for skin divers

MOTOR SWITCH

TOW BAR

PONTOON

Steering for this easily built, slow-motion raft is simply a shove or a foot-flipper kick by the swimmer. The motor is set for about 2 mph, and the skin diver gets a leisurely view of the bottom with minimum effort. Buoyancy lets swimmers rest on the deck

than $100 if you have some lengths of 2x6s and 2x4s around.

Power for the raft is best supplied by one of the newly popular little electric trolling motors, though a tiny gas outboard can also be used. With either, it is wise to fit a wire cage around the propellers as a prop guard so that there will be no chance of divers bumping into blades. All power is shut off, of course, when divers are below the surface. One or two divers can be towed at up to two mph for about two hours per battery charge. Steering is accomplished by the diver angling himself behind the rig. Higher speeds

fun projects

Easy to beach and light enough to be cartopped, the rig can also be unbolted to fit inside a car

Flotation for almost 800 pounds permits passengers, or the craft can be used as a rest raft for divers

would make steering—and sightseeing through your face mask—difficult.

Flotation for the scooter comes from four rotationally molded polyethylene pontoon modules made by Rotocast Plastic Products, 67 N. W. 36th Ave., Miami, Fla. 33147. Two three-foot body sections and two nose sections are required. The body sections and nose sections are about $21 f.o.b. apiece. Rotocast has dealers around the country and can give you the address of the nearest local outlet. Experience in Florida waters indicates the pontoons don't deteriorate and probably have a life of many years. Antifouling paint can be applied if they show signs of barnacle buildup in some coastal waters.

For the model shown, two 5-foot lengths of 2x6 were used for the side stringers. Cross mem-

bers can be three 4-foot lengths of 2x4s. These can be screwed or lagbolted in place, secured with brackets, or special cross-member brackets are available at about $1 each from the pontoon manufacturer. You'll need six. For small motors, the forward 2x4 cross member provides a clamping spot for your power supply. Bolt a section of 2x6 across the front as a motor mount if you need to support a larger outboard.

The size of the afterdeck is optional, depending on your needs. As shown, a battery and equipment storage compartment with top hatch, about 4x3 feet and 1 foot deep can be constructed of ½-inch plywood. Swim fins, masks, snorkels and even wet suits and scuba gear could be carried along in a larger size box.

Some divers prefer simply to rest their 6 or

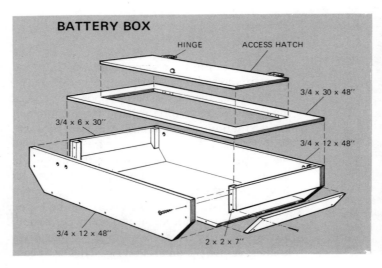

BATTERY BOX

HINGE   ACCESS HATCH

3/4 x 30 x 48''

3/4 x 6 x 30''

3/4 x 12 x 48''

3/4 x 12 x 48''

2 x 2 x 7''

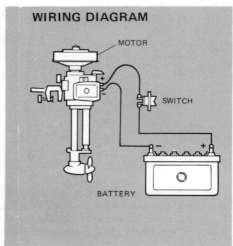

WIRING DIAGRAM

MOTOR

SWITCH

BATTERY

Add more pontoons, and a raft large enough for double-decker sunning or fishing is the result. A houseboat can also be constructed, with the raft serving as the hull

12-volt battery in a simple securing frame on the deck since it is easier to remove than lifting from the storage box for regular charging. Though the battery on deck will be well above water level, a fiberglass battery box, that secures to the deck with nylon tie-down straps, offers more protection from spray. These boxes cost about $5 at marine supply stores.

Most electric outboards come with heavy-duty battery cables and clamp grips. Keep the grips on the cables since you will be disconnecting regularly to charge the battery. Cut into one cable, however, and attach the leads from your on-off switch. This switch is mounted in the middle of your tow-handle grip. The tow handle can be a 12-foot length of aluminum or galvanized ¾ or 1-inch pipe bent into U shape, with wires to the kill switch run inside. We used a switch from a Crowell bilge pump but any waterproof switch should do. It can also be mounted on the back of the storage compartment.

Forward of the decking, a fish net strung between the stringers and cross members will provide a handy catchall for gear or shells and objects brought up from the bottom during a dive. Eyebolts, secured fore and aft, can secure an anchor line or tow lines if the rig is to be pulled along to the diving area behind a larger craft. The pontoons, which are sealed at each end and designed to lock together, provide nearly 800 pounds of flotation and easily support a tired diver who wants to climb up and ride on deck.

Before assembling the components, it is well to paint the wooden parts with colored fiberglass resin or marine paint for waterproofing. The pontoons come in an attractive blue. The rig is light enough for cartopping, but can also be constructed so it can be disassembled by unbolting to fit into a car trunk.

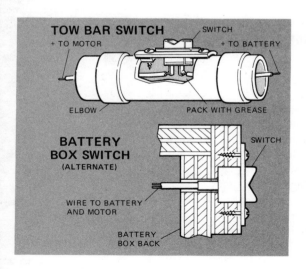

TOW BAR SWITCH
+ TO MOTOR   SWITCH   + TO BATTERY
ELBOW   PACK WITH GREASE

BATTERY BOX SWITCH (ALTERNATE)
SWITCH
WIRE TO BATTERY AND MOTOR
BATTERY BOX BACK

BILL OF MATERIALS	
No.	**Size and Description (Use)**
2	2x6 stock lumber 5' long (stringers)
3	2x4 stock lumber approx. 4' long (cross members)
12'	¾" or 1" aluminum or galvanized pipe (tow bar)
1 sheet	½" marine plywood (deck or storage box)
1 qt.	4-oz. colored fiberglass resin (waterproofing)
1	waterproof on-off switch
4	Pontoon sections
25'	2-wire electric cable (motor switch)
Misc.	assorted screws and $5/16$" lagbolts

A $300 pool table for $100

BY JOHN CAPOTOSTO

With billiards quickly growing as a favorite indoor sport everyone wants a pool table. You can build this sturdy full-size table yourself and save almost $200

■ IF YOU HAVE DONE any shopping lately you know that a pool table is an expensive item to buy. However, if you are good at working with tools you can save almost $200 by building this beauty. Believe it or not, I only spent about $107 to build it, and that includes everything—even the balls and cues. Such hard-to-get items as billiard cloth, cushion rubber and foam padding come in a kit (a source of these necessities for any pool table is given at the end of the article).

This table is well-designed and if constructed

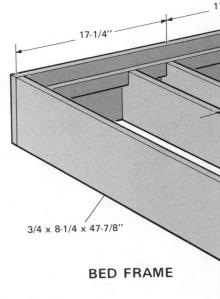

1-3/8''

3/4''

17-1/4''

17-1

3/4 x 8-1/4 x 47-7/8''

BED FRAME

1-1/2''-N
FH SCR

176